Gather Faithfully

Leader's Guide

Gather Faithfully

Inviting Teens into Liturgical Ministries

Leader's Guide

Laure L. Krupp

Saint Mary's Press®

Genuine recycled paper with 10% post-consumer waste. 5113700

The publishing team included Robert Feduccia Jr., development editor; Lorraine Kilmartin, reviewer; Mary Koehler, permissions editor; Dynamic Graphics/Picturequest, cover images; prepress and manufacturing coordinated by the prepublication and production services departments of Saint Mary's Press.

Printed in the United States of America

Printing: 9 8 7 6 5 4 3 2

Year: 2014 13 12 11 10 09 08 07 06

ISBN-13: 978-0-88489-923-5
ISBN-10: 0-88489-923-3

Contents

Introduction

Two Cornerstones: A Vision for Ministry at the Eucharistic Liturgy

The Dance of Liturgy

A champion football team, a ballet production, a choir with perfect four-part harmony, and a Tony award-winning Broadway play: What do these things have in common? They each require that individual efforts be aimed toward the whole, not toward the individual. Similarly, the Eucharistic liturgy is not simply a time for the individual. It is a celebration that requires the entire Body of Christ and is for the entire Body of Christ.

At its best, the Eucharistic liturgy can be described as a beautifully choreographed dance; yet the various pieces of the liturgy can often be planned and prepared for independently of one another. Consideration for the way those pieces are connected to the whole can often be neglected. Readers, extraordinary ministers of Holy Communion, servers, ministers of hospitality, and others are trained to carry out their tasks. However, ensuring that each liturgical minister understands that her or his individual ministry is connected to something more is rarely considered. Flowing through effective liturgical ministry training must be the understanding that each ministry serves the dance that is the Eucharistic liturgy.

Coordinating the Dance

Gather Faithfully: Inviting Teens into Liturgical Ministries is a resource to help you coordinate the liturgical involvement of young people in the liturgy through a comprehensive training program. It is comprehensive because it not only trains the aspiring minister in the skills required but it also forms the young person's spirituality. The complete program contains both a leader's guide and a participant's booklet.

Gather Faithfully: Inviting Teens into Liturgical Ministries, Leader's Guide

This leader's guide will provide you with clear direction for involving young people in the Eucharistic liturgy. However, as the trainer, you might find it helpful to familiarize yourself with the *General Instruction for the Roman Missal* (United States Catholic Conference, Inc., Washington, DC: 2003).

This is the Church's universal document guiding the Eucharistic liturgy. It contains comments and instructions for many of the ministries contained in this leader's guide. It can certainly serve as a cornerstone background document as you begin these sessions. This background can better inform you as you go through the structure of the leader's guide as it develops young people into liturgical ministers.

In this guide you will find the following:

An Introductory Session

This session is for *all* liturgical ministers who will go through the program. The purpose of this session is for the participants to see how their individual part will fit into the whole, at the liturgy and beyond.

Training Sessions

The program will provide training for six ministries: ministry of Reader, extraordinary minister of Holy Communion, ministry of altar server, ministry of hospitality, ministry of sacristan, and ministry of cantor. Each ministry has three sessions:

- Sessions 1 and 2: Personal and spiritual formation for the ministry
- Session 3: Development of practical skills

Continuation

Finally, there is a guide for the ongoing formation of the liturgical ministers.

Gather Faithfully: Inviting Teens into Liturgical Ministries, Participant's Booklet

To accompany the training sessions, there is a participant's booklet. This booklet serves two purposes. First, it serves as a workbook for the training sessions. Much of the training will depend on processes contained in the workbook. It is essential that you have one of these booklets both during your preparation and also during the sessions. It will also be essential for each participant to have a copy of the booklet in order to go through the training program.

Second, the booklet will be the participants' guide for preparing for ministry. It will serve as a reference tool, containing the instructions necessary for confident service. It also contains a guide for spiritually preparing for ministry and a means to reflect on the ministry after the time is past. These guides for preparation and reflection are the last two chapters in the participant's booklet. Please be sure to direct the participants to these chapters.

Transforming the Dancer

Gather Faithfully is more than the practical "how-tos." The larger vision of the program is to transform young people into more faithful disciples of Jesus Christ and for this discipleship to be celebrated in the Eucharistic liturgy. Like the river giving life to the desert, two graces can root the individual in a vision for true worship in Eucharistic liturgy: gift of self and prayer.

1.   **Gift of self.** In liturgical ministry, the minister presents himself or herself to the community, for the community. In much the same way the whole community receives the gifts of bread and wine offered at the Eucharistic liturgy, so, too, the whole community receives the liturgical minister who offers himself or herself in service.

The liturgical minister, called from her or his Baptism as priest, prophet, and king, answers with the ancient words, "Here I am." When God called to Moses from the burning bush, Moses said, "Here I am" (Exodus 3:4). When God called to young Isaiah in the Temple, Isaiah said, "Here am I" (Isaiah 6:8). When God calls the liturgical minister forth to serve his people, she or he responds, "Here I am." They present themselves to God to be a gift for the community.

2. **Prayer.** Liturgy is prayer. In fact it is *the* prayer. In Eucharistic liturgy, the faithful are fully bound together to one another in Jesus Christ, and, in Jesus Christ, they are bound to the Father. The aim of prayer is to bring the person into greater intimacy with the God who loves him or her and to love others more deeply. As adults responsible for being a part of fostering a young person's relationship with God, we are called to model such a relationship.

In order to teach these things, a campus minister or youth minister must search her or his own heart to be more and more authentic in love with the Church's liturgical life. Since we desire young people to see that they do belong in the Church, our own connection to the Eucharistic liturgy must be visible to them. Authenticity is the primary calling card, and authenticity is critical to success.

Proceeding

Self-giving and prayer, skills and spirituality, the dancer and the dance, these images have been used as metaphors for the great call to be a servant at the great Eucharistic banquet. *Gather Faithfully* aims to impact you and your young people to ensure the full, lifelong involvement in the Body of Christ. Saint Paul wrote: "The gifts he gave were that some would be apostles, some prophets, some evangelists, some pastors and teachers, to equip the saints for the work of ministry, for building up the body of Christ" (Ephesians 4:11–12). Gifts are given in order to build up the Body of Christ. The young people you are about to work with possess the gifts necessary to build up the Body and to serve as witnesses to the community. It is an exciting time, indeed.

Guide for Planning

Identifying Youth

> But the LORD said to Samuel, "Do not look on his appearance or on the height of his stature, because I have rejected him; for the LORD does not see as mortals see; they look on the outward appearance, but the LORD looks on the heart."
>
> (1 Samuel 16:7)

Choosing young people to participate in *Gather Faithfully* requires a look at both the practical and the spiritual. The prayerful choice of the campus or youth minister, made in collaboration with other school or parish leaders, may well call a young person out of their "shell" and assist him or her in overcoming self-imposed limitations.

With this in mind, a minister can be faced with a difficult question: how does a trainer know when to accept and when to challenge limitations? For example, it may seem natural to invite a young person with a quiet demeanor to be a sacristan rather than a reader. However, it is possible that the young person has carried the label of *quiet* so long that she or he now defines herself or himself with that label. It is possible that removing the label will reveal a remarkable proclaimer of the word.

The observant trainer looks for small indicators, such as the following:

- comfort in speaking one-on-one with adults
- knowledge of the answers when called on
- acuity for remembering things from one week to the next, such as topics discussed
- respect by peers for thoughts and opinions

In finding a quiet young person who possesses such traits, you might have found a young person ready to be challenged.

As you begin to select young people, look for young people of character in addition to young people of talent. Such young people live as witnesses to the Gospel both within the Eucharistic liturgy and outside of it. These ministries at the Eucharistic liturgy can be a powerful public expression of faith in Jesus Christ. It will be important not to have any stumbling blocks that would prevent the full impact of this witness.

As you begin to assemble the possible participants, it is important to do so in consultation with other adults in your community. In a school, confer with teachers who can offer fair, unbiased opinions. Many brilliant students have not been invited into the National Honor Society because of inappropriate behavior, despite their academic ability. Other adults who know the young people well, teachers, or catechists, will be able to alert you to any public behavior that may not be congruent with public ministry. This is a careful line to walk. There is the risk that a young person could be unjustly excluded. Such decisions should be approached with prayerful wisdom.

Incorporating Adults

Other adults in the school or parish community may be willing to assist with liturgical ministries training. Considering that there are a total of twenty sessions, it will be vital for the program for you to identify other adults to assist you. You are urged to be discerning when choosing which adults to incorporate into a training program. The offer ought not to warrant an unreflected "yes." The trainer must ask the same questions of potential adult assistants as he or she does for potential youth candidates:

- Does this person have a rapport with young people?
- Does he or she listen well?
- Does she or he enjoy helping young people?

As an advocate for young people, it is the trainer's job to do all that he or she can do to ensure a positive, creative, respectful, and reverent training environment. Adults who are respectful of young people, who love the Eucharistic liturgy and are excited to be the bridge to help young people discover its richness are good candidates to assist with the training of young people for liturgical ministries.

Planning for Training

To find our starting point, we must know our ending point. The hope of *Gather Faithfully* is that at its end, young people will be integrated into the liturgical life of the Church as liturgical ministers. The purpose of *Gather Faithfully* is to equip young people to serve alongside their brothers and sisters regardless of age. As the Catholic Church is a universal Church, it is a rich reflection of the Church's nature to have a sixteen-year-old distributing Holy Communion next to a sixty-year-old.

As you have set your vision, identified the right young people and adult assistants, you may find the following will help you in your preparation:

- Check with your diocesan worship office to ensure that your diocese permits young people to be involved in the liturgical ministries in which you hope to train young people.
- Check with your chaplain, sacramental minister, or pastor. Certain local policies regarding teenagers and liturgical ministries may be in place.
- Determine the right people from the school community or parish to involve. The school's music teacher and the leaders of liturgical ministries

at your parish are valuable assets to your training.

- Consult with teachers, administrators, and peer leaders in a school. In a parish, seek input from the parish staff, catechists, and youth leaders to see which young people might be good candidates for liturgical ministry.
- How will the young people be invited to take part in *Gather Faithfully*? Meet face to face with the young person if at all possible.
- Determine how, when, and where training will take place. Each of the six ministries has three training sessions. For a school, the sessions were designed so that they could be conducted during lunch or activity periods. At a parish, the sessions could be held on three consecutive evenings.
- Gather pertinent information from your particular community. For example, principles of serving at the Eucharistic liturgy are laid out in *Gather Faithfully*. However, it will also be important to incorporate school or parish customs into your training.
- What role will your chaplain, sacramental minister, or pastor play during the training sessions? He may wish to teach a session, or he may wish to observe only.
- Read through all the sessions before beginning any training. Good training is a result of good planning.

An Important Note

As you seek to involve others in training liturgical ministers, one caution is in order. Appropriate and healthy relationship boundaries are real concerns anytime adults interact with young people. In light of heightened public awareness of and attention to child protection issues, we must ensure that a safe and healthy relationship is maintained between the adults and the young people who will spend time together. In fact, all dioceses have specific guidelines for adults who work with young people. Criminal background checks, references, and special training for those engaged in ministry are some of the tools that ensure the quality of the adults working with our young people. Check the diocesan requirements concerning criminal background checks and the use of volunteer covenants.

In ministry with youth, there are several practical guidelines to keep in mind:

- Providing a young person with an alcoholic beverage, tobacco, or drugs is never allowed.
- Touching must be age-appropriate and based on the need of the training session and not on the need of the adult. Physical contact must be avoided when an adult is alone with a young person.
- Adults should not be alone with a young person in a residence, sleeping facility, locker room, restroom, dressing facility, or other closed room or isolated area that is inappropriate to a ministry relationship. Adults must always meet with young people in visible and accessible areas. One-on-one

meetings with a young person are best held in a public area.

- It is always a safe practice to have two adults in the area where youth are present.
- Driving alone with a young person should be avoided.
- Engaging in physical discipline of a young person is unacceptable.
- Taking an overnight trip alone with a young person from the parish or school community who is not a member of your immediate family is prohibited.
- Topics, vocabulary, recordings, films, games, or the use of computer software or any other form of personal interaction or entertainment that could not be used comfortably in the presence of parents must not be used with young people. Sexually explicit or pornographic material is prohibited.
- If anyone (adult or minor) abuses a young person in your presence, take appropriate steps to immediately intervene and to provide a safe environment for the young person. Report the misconduct to the appropriate authority in accord with the diocesan guidelines.
- Be proactive in identifying young people who may be vulnerable or at-risk for unhealthy relationships. Adults can have a very positive influence on young people by sharing the message of how important youth are in God's eyes, and that they are created with dignity. This can reduce the possibility of them falling into the traps of those who tell them love is just physical.

Piecing Together the Puzzle

Overview

Session Goals

- To bring understanding concerning how the individual pieces of the liturgy connect to the whole
- To have the participants understand that they are vital members of the Body of Christ

Materials

- ❑ a candle
- ❑ matches or a lighter
- ❑ a photograph of the school or church and a photo of students or parish youth, enlarged to poster size, then cut into "jigsaw puzzle" pieces
- ❑ two pieces of poster board, large enough to hold the completed photographs
- ❑ bibles, one for each participant
- ❑ A copy of resource 1, "Quotes from the Acts of the Apostles 3:1–10," cut apart with each quote on a separate slip of paper

Opening Prayer

Gather the participants around a candle. Select a leader and a reader from among the participants and give one participant the matches or lighter. Ask the reader to prepare to proclaim Ephesians 4:1–6.

Leader: We have arrived physically. Now let's take a moment to arrive in our hearts and spirits as well. (Allow for a few moments of silence.)

Leader: As a reminder that we all received the light of faith at our Baptism, we will light the candle and begin. (At this point, the participant with the matches or lighter may light the candle.)

Leader: Let's begin together, in the name of the Father, and of the Son, and of the Holy Spirit.

Reading: Ephesians 4:1–6

Leader: LORD our God, and Father of all, it is you who calls us together and gives us purpose. It is you who brings together our gifts and our hearts.

Unite us as a community of believers, that through our ministries, the people of God may experience your touch when we gather to worship. We make this prayer in the name of Jesus our LORD. Amen.

Activity

1. Divide the participants into ten groups. Ten groups is the optimal number for this session; if this is too large of a number for your group, please create smaller groups. After the participants are in their groups, prompt them with the following to help facilitate a conversation:

- Please go around and introduce yourselves. After the introductions, share with each other the answers to these questions about teams:

- What is your all-time favorite team? This could be a sports team, music group, or any other ensemble.

- When have you most felt like you were part of a successful team?

After allowing time for the participants to talk, distribute the bibles and invite them to turn to the Acts of the Apostles 3:1–10. Invite a young person to read the passage.

2. After the passage has been read, distribute one quote from the resource to each of the groups. Allow the groups enough time to respond to their question or statement.

3. Invite a person from each group to read their question or statement to the larger group and to share some of the responses provided.

4. After each group has offered their thoughts, draw out the following points:

- The Scripture passage from the Acts of the Apostles serves as a reminder that we are called to be ministers at times we don't expect.

- These unexpected times to be God's witnesses originate from our participation in the Eucharistic liturgy.

- In liturgy, we bring our life experiences to our prayer and leave that prayer ready to be a witness to the Gospel of Jesus Christ at every moment of the day.

5. After offering these reflections on the Scripture, distribute all but four of the pieces to the puzzles among the young people. Place the two pieces of poster board in the middle of the room and instruct the young people to put together the puzzles.

6. After all but the four pieces are in place, offer the following words to the young people:

- The Eucharistic liturgy is a harmonized work of God's people that becomes a gift to God.

- In this coordinated harmonized work, every ministry and every person is important. (At this point, place the remaining pieces into the puzzles.)

- The ministries we are about to be trained in are absolutely necessary for the liturgy to be a complete celebration.

- In liturgical ministry, we are going to prepare our individual ministry toward the goal of building up our entire school or parish community.

- As we go forward into these ministries, we should be changed into people who are ready to minister outside of the Eucharistic liturgy as well—ready to be a witness to the Gospel at any place or at any time.

7. To conclude the session, gather the participants in a circle and read Acts of the Apostles 3:1–10 once again. Offer this closing prayer:

Our savior and our healer, we do not have much. But you take what we have and make it into something far greater than we can imagine. As we have answered your call to be liturgical ministers, may we grow spiritually and grow closer to you. May we see ourselves as members of your body and see that we all have gifts to share. Bless us, our ministries, and the community we will serve. We ask this through Christ the LORD. Amen.

Quotes from the Acts
of the Apostles 3:1–10

- "Peter and John. . ." Ministry is best when we work together with other people of faith. Share with other people in your small group a time when you worked on something that became better because you joined forces with another person.

- ". . . at the hour of prayer, at three o'clock." Life for the man at the gate changed because Peter and John were going to pray. When have you offered God's comfort to someone in need?

- "People would lay him daily at the gate." The man had been placed at the gate by someone who hoped the man would get what he needed there. What are some things that young people need from the Church?

- "Peter looked intently at him." Instead of simply emptying out his pockets, Peter took a moment and really looked at the man at the gate. Peter didn't look at the problem; he considered the person. When have you really felt listened to when you have had a problem?

- "I have no silver or gold." Peter recognized that he didn't have what the man was looking for. Have you ever felt like you don't have anything to offer the Church? Explain.

- ". . . but what I have I give you;" Instead of reaching into his pockets, Peter reached into his heart. As a teenager with limited resources, what do you think you have to give to God and to the Church?

- "And he took him by the right hand and raised him up;" Take a moment, and imagine friends or family members who have struggled. Describe a time when you have reached out and helped someone in need.

- ". . . immediately his feet and ankles were made strong." When we make a response in faith, God is ready to meet us. Have you ever seen a miracle or had a prayer answered in a way you had hoped? Explain.

- ". . . he entered the temple with them." Once the man at the gate experienced the touch of God, his instinctive reaction was to go and pray with Peter and John. Have you seen instances when prayers have been answered but then God was forgotten about? When God answers prayers, why do you think it is hard to remember to go back and thank him?

- "All the people saw him walking and praising God." When have you been impressed by someone's faith or relationship with God?

Ministry of Reader

Session 1

Overview

Session Goals

- To help the participants learn how to prepare scriptural texts for proclamation at liturgies
- To familiarize the participants with preparation techniques for proclaiming scriptural texts

Materials

- ❑ *Lectionaries* or bibles, one for each participant. It is encouraged that you use a variety of readings.

- ❑ a candle

- ❑ *Gather Faithfully* Participant's Booklet

- ❑ a biblical dictionary, for looking up the pronunciation of difficult words

Activity

Opening Prayer

Prior to the participants' arrival have a *Lectionary* or a Bible on a table in the center of a prayer circle with a lighted candle next to it. The prayer will require a leader and a reader. Have the *Lectionary* or the Bible open to one of the following passages:

- 2 Timothy 3:14–17
- Isaiah 55:10–11
- 2 Timothy 4:1–5
- Matthew 5:14–19

Ask one of the participants to prepare to read one of these passages.

Gather the participants in a circle for prayer and encourage them to observe a moment of silence in preparation for prayer. After the moment of silence begin the prayer.

Leader: Let us begin in the name of the Father, and of the Son, and of the Holy Spirit.

All: Amen.

Leader: Let us listen to the word of God.

The reader should read the passage selected.

Note: In order for the participants to become comfortable with the *Lectionary*, it is encouraged that the reader uses the *Lectionary* in proclamation.

Leader: Gracious and loving God, Jesus your Son, proclaimed your word in the Temple. Bless us as we gather to prepare for the ministry of reader. We ask this of you, Father, in Jesus, your Son and with the power of the Holy Spirit. Amen.

Activity

1. Once the prayer has been completed, inform the participants that you would like for them to think about the characteristics of a good actor. To aid in this reflection, lead a discussion prompted by the following questions:

   o What makes actors good actors?

   o How do they remember their lines?

   o How do they decide what emotions they are supposed to express?

2. It would be important to share the following points about the craft of acting. Good acting comes from the following elements:

- Good actors have the gift to act.
- Good actors practice their lines.
- Good actors' emotions come from the script and what's happening in the scene.
- Good actors listen to what a director tells them.
- Good actors rehearse and rehearse and rehearse.

After making the previous points, address the participant with these or similar words:

   o In some ways, reading from Scripture is like acting. The words you read are not yours. They came from people who were inspired by God to tell about his presence with them and his instructions for following Jesus the Christ. When we serve as a reader during the liturgy, we are trying to share God's word, God's love, and his eternal message with our brothers and sisters in faith. If we are to be God's voice, the mouths through which God speaks, then each of us ought to do as best we can. This session will begin to lead us through some methods of preparation to help us proclaim the word with skills worthy of God's word.

At this point, ask the participants to turn to the sections titled "The Bible" and "Understanding the Passage," starting on page 8 in the *Gather Faithfully* Participant's Booklet. Review these two sections and talk about each aspect with the participant.

3. Divide the group into smaller groups of two or three participants. Once they are in their groups, assign the various readings from the Opening Prayer section to the groups. As you make the assignments within this step, do not assign the same reading to each group unless you think it would be important to hear the same reading repeated.

Ask the participants to prepare the reading in the manner described in step one of "Understanding the Passage" in the *Gather Faithfully* Participant's Booklet. Each participant should read the text to himself or herself. Next they should look up unknown words. If you were able to obtain a biblical dictionary, remind the participants that it is available.

After they have completed step one, invite them to share their reflections with the others in their group.

4. Once the groups have had a chance to discuss the readings have them move on to step two. The group should create a summary of no more than three sentences.

5. When the work is complete, ask the participants to gather again as a large group. Invite one member of each group to share their group summary. Inquire about difficult words they found.

6. Instruct the groups to reassemble in the groups of two or three used in the previous steps. This time they are to proceed to step three in "Understanding the Passage," in the *Gather Faithfully* Participant's Booklet. Each is to read the passage silently and then take turns proclaiming the Scripture to the others in the small group. As a group they should determine what words or phrases need to be emphasized in order for the meaning of the passage to be fully revealed. They will then choose a person who will proclaim the reading to the large group.

7. After each group has completed the work of step three in "Understanding the Passage," in the *Gather Faithfully* Participant's Booklet, invite them to return to the large group. Now randomly call on a group to select a representative to read the Scripture passage they were assigned.

8. Close with the following prayer:

> Lord God,
> in Jesus, you gave us the Word made flesh.
> Fill our hearts with a great love for your word.
> Help us to know how important it is to read your word,
> to spend time in preparation
> if we are to share it with others.
> We ask this in your name. Amen.

Ministry of Reader

Session 2

Overview

Session Goals

- The participants will understand the importance of tone of voice in communicating meaning.
- The participants will learn skills in preparing to proclaim the Scriptures at the liturgy.

Materials

- ❑ a candle
- ❑ matches or a lighter
- ❑ *Gather Faithfully* Participant's Booklet
- ❑ copies of resource 2, "The Power of Tone," one for each group of two or three
- ❑ pens or pencils, one for each participant
- ❑ a CD of instrumental music
- ❑ a CD player

Session Activity

Opening Prayer

Gather the participants around a table with the candle. Select a leader and a reader from among the participants and give one participant the matches or lighter. Ask the reader to prepare to proclaim John 1:1–5.

Leader: We have arrived physically. Now let's take a moment to arrive in our hearts and spirits as well. (Allow for a few moments of silence.)

Leader: As a reminder that the word of God is a lamp for our feet and a light for our path, we will light the candle and begin. (At this point, the participant with the matches or lighter may light the candle.)

Leader: Let's begin together, in the name of the Father, and of the Son, and of the Holy Spirit.

Leader: Jesus, you are the Word made flesh. It was through you that the Father said, "Let there be light" (Genesis 1:3). Let us find you in the words proclaimed here today.

Reading: John 1:1–5 (from page 11 in the *Gather Faithfully* Participant's Booklet).

Leader: Jesus, God's word revealed, use our voices to reveal your presence and power among us. May all who hear these words come to know you more fully. We make this prayer in your most holy name. Amen.

Activity

In this activity, the participants will discover how the tone of one's voice conveys meaning.

1. To begin this session, it would be important to emphasize the way in which reading God's word in the liturgy is comparable to a conversation. It would be helpful to begin a discussion with the participants with these or similar questions:

- As we know from conversation, it isn't just what you say, but how you say it.

- What are some ways that tone of voice changes something nice into something insulting?

- What are some ways that tone of voice can make something, for example, a piece of constructive criticism, easier to hear?

2. After garnering specific examples from the participants, make the following points about tone of voice:

- Tone can confirm or contradict the message.
- Tone tells the listener how we would like them to receive our words.
- Tone tells the listener what we think is important about what we are saying.

3. Divide the group into four small groups. Give each small group one section of resource 2, "The Power of Tone." If possible, try to ensure that the groups don't realize that they are all working with the same sentence.

- **<u>YOU</u>** are my friend.
- You **<u>ARE</u>** my friend.
- You are **<u>MY</u>** friend.
- You are my **<u>FRIEND</u>**.

Instruct the participants to turn to the section titled "It's All in How You Say It," on page 11 of the *Gather Faithfully* Participant's Booklet. They should then look at their sentence from resource 2; the underlined word is to communicate the primary meaning of the sentence. It is the "tone" word. Instruct the participants to make up a scenario that includes this sentence, with its assigned emphasis, and then write it in the space provided in "It's All in How You Say It," on page 11 of the *Gather Faithfully* Participant's Booklet.

Allow the participants five minutes to complete the exercise.

4. Have each small group present their sentence, with its emphasis, then the scenario they wrote.

Discuss as a large group the following points:

- Since Scripture doesn't come with underlined words, it is important to know how each word and each sentence fits into the whole.
- Each sentence in the text supports the overall theme. By determining the overall theme, we better understand what words to "underline" with our voice.
- When we are not familiar with the theme of the reading, our proclamation becomes a string of sentences, and it is difficult for the congregation to connect them together.
- One can find many different themes in a passage. How do you know which to emphasize? Look at other readings and see if there is a corresponding theme. Call your priest to see if he would like a particular emphasis to the reading. Through such consultation and through your own prayerful reflection, the meaning will emerge.

5. It may be helpful to have quiet, instrumental music playing in the background during this exercise. Ask the participants to spread about the room with the Participant's Booklet and a pen or pencil, and inform them that they will go through the process described in the section titled "Preparing to Serve as a Reader at the Liturgy," on pages 11–12 of the Participant's Booklet. Instruct them to do the following:

- Please pray with me in your hearts: "Holy Spirit, it is you who reveals God's truth and meaning. Shine your light on these holy and ancient words that they may come alive for us again today, and we may find your truth. We ask this Christ our LORD. Amen."

- Turn to page 11 of the Participant's Booklet and read the Scripture passage to yourself (John 1:1–5).

- Continue to read and reread the passage. When you are ready, make a summary of the passage in a way that makes sense to you under the section titled "What Is the Word Saying?"

- Now return to the passage, and underline the words and phrases that help you emphasize the theme.

6. After allowing time for the exercise, ask the young people to find a partner. The partners should then read their interpretation of the passage to each other. Emphasize that the one listening should listen, not think ahead to compare their thoughts or interpretation.

At the end of the reading, the listener should share with the reader the words that seemed to be underlined, and what theme arose from the reader's proclamation. The reader should compare what his or her partner heard with what he or she intended to emphasize. Allow time for the roles to be reversed.

7. Ask for a volunteer to read to the large group. After this reading, ask the group to give the reader feedback—what words or phrases did she or he underline with her or his voice? Point to the meaning the group has gained from the prayerful reflection of different people. Encourage the participants to practice their reading in front of someone when preparing to proclaim for the liturgy of the Mass. If that isn't possible, encourage them to read out loud to themselves.

8. Gather the group in a large circle, instructing them to bring their Participant's Booklets with them. Ask each person to choose three words or phrases that they have underlined that they will emphasize when they read aloud the passage. Tell the participants that you will lead an opening prayer, then starting with the person on your right, each of them will read the words or phrases that they have chosen. Ask them to read clearly, to proclaim the words, using their voice to communicate meaning. When the circle gets back to you, you will lead a concluding prayer:

Leader: O LORD our God, your holy word is like a diamond. The more we look at it, the more beauty we see in its depths. Hear now the word we have found this day.

Note: Prompt the young people to begin.

Leader: Thank you, Holy Spirit, for revealing the word of God to us. Keep the ears of our heart open that we may continually see the beauty that lies at the depths of God's word. We make this prayer in the name of Jesus our LORD, who is the Word made flesh. Amen.

The Power of Tone

YOU are my friend.

You **ARE** my friend.

You are **MY** friend.

You are my **FRIEND**.

Ministry of Reader

Session 3

Overview

Session Goals

- The participants will learn how to prepare a Scripture reading by the pauses, punctuation, and phrasing contained in the Scripture passage.
- The participants will learn the practical preparation of proclaiming at the liturgy.

Materials

- ☐ a candle
- ☐ matches or a lighter
- ☐ *Gather Faithfully* Participant's Booklet
- ☐ pens or pencils, one for each participant

Trainer's Preparation

General Instruction on the Roman Missal provides the Church with the universal guidelines for the Eucharistic liturgy. It could be helpful to read paragraphs 46 through 90 as background material on the structure of the liturgy, and paragraphs 194 through 198, "The Duties of the Lector."

Session Activity

Opening Prayer

Gather the participants. Select a leader and a reader from among the participants and give one participant the matches or lighter. Ask the reader to prepare Romans 8:31–39.

Leader: We have arrived physically. Now let's take a moment to arrive in our hearts and spirits as well. (Allow for a few moments of silence.)

Leader: As a reminder that the word of God is a lamp for our feet and a light for our path, we will light the candle and begin. (At this point, the participant with the matches or lighter may light the candle.)

Leader: Let's begin together, in the name of the Father, and of the Son, and of the Holy Spirit.

Leader: O Word of God, be with us, we pray, as we gather with your holy word. Open our eyes to see you, our hearts to receive you, and our minds to understand you more fully.

Reading: Romans 8:31–39 (from page 12 in the *Gather Faithfully* Participant's Booklet).

Leader: Father, all you do in our lives is out of love for us. May our proclamation of your holy word lead others to fuller understanding of your great love for us. We make this prayer through Christ our LORD.

Activity

1. Review sessions one and two and introduce this session in the following manner by asking the following questions and making the following comments:

○ What are the main points that you want to remember?

○ So far, what are the things you think of as important to being a reader?

○ In sessions one and two, we have spoken about how to discover meaning in the Scripture passage. We talked about using our voices to underline, or give emphasis to, words that will aid the congregation in understanding the Scripture passage. In this session we will begin by looking at the importance of using punctuation cues.

2. After the introduction, ask the participants to turn to Romans 8:31–39 on page 12 in the *Gather Faithfully* Participant's Booklet and invite them to read the passage aloud. After the reading is complete, instruct the participants in the following manner:

○ This is a difficult reading to proclaim, and it is a difficult reading for the congregation to follow. When proclaiming readings such as this, preparation becomes even more critical. Review the instructions titled "Preparing the Punctuation," on pages 12–13 in the *Gather Faithfully* Participant's Booklet. Following the instructions in that section, prepare the reading from Romans.

3. After allowing time for the participants to mark the passage as instructed, gather with them in the community's worship space where they can practice proclaiming the reading. As you gather in the community's worship space, instruct the participants in the local custom of approaching the ambo. For example if the Blessed Sacrament is present, instruct the participants to genuflect. If it is not, instruct them to reverence the altar with a profound bow.

Refer the participants to the "Preparation Guide and Evaluation" section on pages 13–14 of the *Gather Faithfully* Participant's Booklet. Then instruct them in the following manner:

- The ministry of reader is integral to the liturgy. The Church says that Christ is present in the liturgy in four ways: the prayer and singing of the people, the Eucharist, the priest, *and* in the Word. Your proclamation should make it obvious that Christ is present in your proclamation.

- Imagine you are Christ's spokesperson at a formal banquet. You should arrive early at the banquet and should be dressed for a dignified event. (Acceptable attire is usually set by local standards. While all attire should be modest, take the opportunity to instruct the participants on your community's standard for proper attire.)

- How would Christ speak to those gathered? He would stand straight and speak clearly. His voice would fill the room. Do not think that you must only project to the microphone. Rather, think that you must project to the person in the back row. Memorize the introduction to the reading and the first sentence. In doing this, you can maintain eye contact with the congregation.

- Do not start your sentences slowly and then speed up as you go. Maintain a deliberate pace and say all of the words clearly and at the same speed. Refer to the punctuation cues you made in preparation for the reading. Remember, you are proclaiming a meaning, not just words. Recitation is saying words on a page. Proclaiming is conveying the meaning with the feeling intended in the passage.

- Do not appear as though you cannot wait to get down from the ambo. Say, "The Word of the LORD" clearly and do not walk away. As a rule of thumb, pray "Glory be to the Father, and to the Son, and to the Holy Spirit . . ." to yourself and then step down. You want the liturgy to go at a pace that allows the word of God to soak into the congregation.

After these instructions, ask for a volunteer who is willing to receive feedback to proclaim the Scripture passage. The feedback will be based on the applicable parts of the "Preparation Guide and Evaluation" section on pages 13–14 of the *Gather Faithfully* Participant's Booklet.

4. Take the volunteer and walk the participant through the following points that are detailed in "Duties of the Reader" from *General Instruction for the Roman Missal*, paragraphs 194 through 198:

- In the procession, the reader may carry the Book of the Gospels, but not the *Lectionary*. The Book of the Gospels should be slightly elevated as it is carried.

- As the reader approaches the altar in the procession, the reader should genuflect or bow (depending on the presence of the Blessed Sacrament) and then place the Book of the Gospels on the altar.
- When it is time for the reading, the reader will reverently approach the ambo; however, *General Instruction for the Roman Missal* indicates he or she is not to genuflect during the liturgy (see paragraph number 274).
- The reader should slowly and confidently approach the ambo and read the Scripture confidently. Allow the reader also to practice coming down from the ambo according to the instructions cited above.

After the participant has proclaimed the reading, allow the others to provide feedback to her or him.

5. Allow for as many participants as possible to practice their reading and to receive feedback from their peers and from you.

6. Close with the following prayer:

O LORD our God, with your voice, you said, "'Let there be light'" (Genesis 1:3). Your words have power to create, to restore, and to heal. LORD, as we proclaim your words, empower us with your Holy Spirit that all who hear may find power, that they may be restored and healed. We make this prayer in the name of Jesus our LORD. Amen.

Extraordinary Minister of Holy Communion

Session 1

Overview

Session Goals

- To better understand the Body of Christ as a model of the Church
- To better understand the Eucharistic elements as the Body of Christ

Materials

- ☐ a candle
- ☐ matches or a lighter
- ☐ *Gather Faithfully* Participant's Booklet
- ☐ pens or pencils, one for each participant
- ☐ construction paper of different colors, two pieces per person
- ☐ bottles of glue, not glue sticks
- ☐ markers of different colors, at least one for each participant
- ☐ a CD of instrumental music or quiet, uplifting music
- ☐ a CD player
- ☐ small candles, one for each participant

Session Activity

Opening Prayer

Gather the participants around a candle. Select a leader and a reader from among the participants and give one participant the matches or lighter. Ask the reader to prepare to proclaim 1 Corinthians 12:12–20.

Leader: We have arrived physically. Now let's take a moment to arrive in our hearts and spirits as well. (Allow for a few moments of silence.)

Leader: As a reminder that we, though many, are one Body with Jesus Christ, we will light the candle and begin. (At this point, the participant with the matches or lighter may light the candle.)

Leader: Let's begin together, in the name of the Father, and of the Son, and of the Holy Spirit.

Leader: At the Eucharist, we pray to be filled with the Holy Spirit and to be made into one Body, one spirit in Christ. Let us listen prayerfully to God's word.

Reading: 1 Corinthians 12:12–20 (from page 15 in the *Gather Faithfully* Participant's Booklet).

Leader: O loving God, through our Baptism, we have become joined with you in the Body of Christ: Jesus and our brothers and sisters. Strengthen our bonds, heal all that divides us, and turn our hearts toward you and each other. We pray this in the name of your son, our LORD Jesus Christ. Amen.

Activity

1. Invite the young people to spread around the room and provide each person with two sheets of construction paper of differing colors. Also provide a few different colored markers. When the participants have settled into a spot around the room with their paper and markers, begin the instrumental CD.

2. Ask each person to choose one piece of paper. On that paper, instruct the participants to write the things that make them unique by answering the questions from the section titled, "What Makes Me Unique?" on pages 15–16 in the *Gather Faithfully* Participant's Booklet. Encourage them to think deeply about the questions and to write their true thoughts, but let them know that their answers will be shared with others. Also, ask them to write big and to decorate their paper as they write.

   o   How do your friends describe you?

   o   What three qualities are you most proud of?

   o   What are your hobbies, your skills, your interests?

   o   What do you care passionately about?

   o   What do you daydream about?

   o   Draw shapes to symbolize the things about you that you are less proud of. Use symbols so that only you know to what you are referring.

3. After allowing time for the young people to complete the questions, ask them to set aside that paper and to get their second piece. On this piece

of paper, instruct the participants to write the things that make Jesus unique by answering the questions titled "What Makes Jesus Unique?" on page 16 in the *Gather Faithfully* Participant's Booklet.

- How do you describe Jesus?

- What three qualities of Jesus's do you most admire?

- What are Jesus's interests?

- What does Jesus care passionately about?

- What do you think Jesus daydreams about?

4. When it seems that most young people are finished, instruct the participants to glue the two pieces of paper together with the writing facing outward. When everyone has finished gluing the pieces of paper together, read the following passage from John 17:20–21.

> "I ask not only on behalf of these, but also on behalf of those who will believe in me through their word, that they may all be one. As you, Father, are in me and I am in you, may they also be in us, so that the world may believe that you have sent me."

- You and I are united with Jesus just as Jesus is united with the Father.

- Look at your pieces of paper. They are so joined together that it is difficult to distinguish the two.

- Hold up the paper that you put together before the session.

- In our Baptism you and I became so joined with Jesus that our souls will always carry his image, no matter what! We retain our vibrant color, but the imprint made on us at Baptism will always identify us with Christ.

- When we remain in union with Jesus, we are also in union with one another. We are joined with the entire Body of Christ.

5. Invite the participants to turn to page 17 of the *Gather Faithfully* Participant's Booklet and look for the section titled "The Body of Christ." Once they are there, ask them to go around the room with their Participant's Booklet and read other's descriptions of themselves from the section "What Makes Me Unique." Under the section titled "The Body of Christ," they are to write down anything they particularly like or anything that particularly struck them. After they have made their way around the room, invite the participants to turn the papers over to the side that describes Jesus. The participants should again make their way around the room and continue writing based on the words on the side of the paper that describes Jesus.

6. After they have had an opportunity to write their comments, instruct the participants in these or similar words:

- There is a salient point from the movie *Remember the Titans* (2000, 113 minutes, rated PG). In that film a high school football team is about to play a playoff game that will determine who will play for the championship. In the locker room before the game, a team member points out that none of the individuals is perfect, but together they make the perfect team. The Church's impact on the world today would be dramatically different if we truly believed that we are joined with Jesus and that he becomes available to us in the Eucharist.

- As you distribute the body and blood of Christ at the liturgy, you will stand fully joined to Jesus. From that union, he will give his body and blood once more. His is the hand that will lift the consecrated bread and through your voice he will say, "The Body of Christ" or "The Blood of Christ." Jesus Christ himself reaches out through your hands and your voice to give himself to the Body of Christ in Holy Communion.

- As the presence of Christ changes the bread into his sacred body and the wine into his precious blood, so too his presence changes us. As sacred as the consecrated bread, so too is the extraordinary minister of Holy Communion joined with Jesus in the Body of Christ.

7. Gather the participants in a circle and close with the following prayer:

> O God, our light and our hope, you call us to perfect union with yourself. Help us to let our light shine as a member of this Body. For when we are joined with Jesus, nothing can put our light out. We make this prayer in the name of Jesus, who made us one Body. Amen.

Extraordinary Minister of Holy Communion

Session 2

Overview

Session Goals

- To introduce the participants to a proper disposition of service during the Eucharistic liturgy
- To help the participants identify themselves as gifted people that Jesus calls into service of the Church

Materials

- ❑ a candle
- ❑ matches or a lighter
- ❑ *Gather Faithfully* Participant's Booklet
- ❑ pens or pencils, one for each participant
- ❑ several small baskets, one for every four to six participants
- ❑ one larger basket
- ❑ index cards, six for each participant
- ❑ a CD of instrumental music
- ❑ a CD player
- ❑ bibles, one for each participant

Session Activity

Opening Prayer

Gather the participants around a candle. Select a leader and a reader from among the participants and give one participant the matches or lighter. Ask the reader to prepare to proclaim John 6:32–34.

Leader: We have arrived physically. Now let's take a moment to arrive in our hearts and spirits as well. (Allow for a few moments of silence.)

Leader: As a reminder that we, though many, are one Body with Jesus Christ, we will light the candle and begin. (At this point, the participant with the matches or lighter may light the candle.)

Leader: Let's begin together, in the name of the Father, and of the Son, and of the Holy Spirit.

Reading: John 6:32–34 (from page 17 in the *Gather Faithfully* Participant's Booklet).

Leader: LORD our God, you held back nothing from your people, but gave us everything in your son Jesus and in the most holy Eucharist. Help us to hold back nothing from you but to give ourselves fully, without reserve. We ask this through Christ our LORD. Amen.

Activity

1. As the participants gather, ask them to turn to the section titled "The Proper Disposition," on page 17 in the *Gather Faithfully* Participant's Booklet. Read this aloud as they follow along. After reading, make the following comments:

   ○ The Church urges everyone who participates in the Eucharistic liturgy to worship with "the proper disposition." This is especially true for those who will be the community's servants at the liturgy. During this session, we will explore how we can foster such a proper disposition.

2. Divide the participants into groups of four to six people. Distribute the index cards, six per participant, and place a small basket in the middle of each group.

3. Instruct the participants to write on separate index cards the responses to the questions and prompts in the section titled "Giving Myself to God," on pages 17–18 in the *Gather Faithfully* Participant's Booklet. After allowing time for them to write their thoughts, invite them to share them with the other members of the group as they feel comfortable.

4. Once each person has had a chance to share the reflections, ask a participant to pray aloud the "Prayer of Abandonment," on page 18 in the *Gather Faithfully* Participant's Booklet. After the prayer has been prayed, ask the participants to complete the statements that follow and share their answers with their small group.

5. After allowing time for discussion, read the story of the feeding of the five thousand people from John 6:3–11. Then address the participants with these or similar words:

   ○ Feeding the large crowd was a miracle. But in order for that miracle to happen, another miracle had to happen first. Someone had to give

Jesus all the food that they had. Five loaves and two fish would have been too large a meal for a boy. Clearly, he had enough to share with others, but he probably never dreamed that his gift would feed a large crowd. Perhaps the first miracle of the day was that the boy who gave Jesus the five loaves and two fish didn't regard his gift as too small to help; instead, he simply gave his gift.

○ Jesus never considers our gift of self too small. It is always enough. He doesn't ask for our gift of self to be perfect, he just asks for us to present it to him, to surrender ourselves without reserve and with boundless confidence.

6. Begin the instrumental CD and ask the young people to pick up their index cards, setting aside the card with their name on it. Ask them to place the other five cards into the basket in the middle of their group. Let them know that neither you nor anyone else will read the cards. They should do so one card at a time. As they place each card in the basket, invite them to pray to themselves, "Father, I abandon myself into your hands." After they have completed their prayers, invite them to bring the card with their name on it and gather around the candle. Ask one person from each group to bring their group's basket forward, pour it into the large basket that you have placed by the candle and address the participants.

○ Now as a sign that we want to abandon ourselves wholly into the hands as Jesus Christ, as he wholly gave himself to us, without reserve, I invite you to place the card with your name on it into the basket.

○ LORD, receive our five loaves and two fish today as a gift of ourselves, as a sign that we want to give ourselves without reserve, and with boundless confidence.

Extraordinary Minister of Holy Communion

Session 3

Overview

Session Goals

- To learn the practical steps of approaching the altar to receive Holy Communion, including how to handle the Communion vessels, to distribute Holy Communion, and to return the vessels
- To learn the particular nuances of serving as an extraordinary minister of Holy Communion for the local Eucharistic community

Materials

- ❑ a candle
- ❑ matches or a lighter
- ❑ *Gather Faithfully* Participant's Booklet
- ❑ pens or pencils, one for each participant
- ❑ sacred vessels
- ❑ the community's worship space
- ❑ unconsecrated Communion elements (hosts and wine)

Trainer Preparation

General Instruction on the Roman Missal provides the Church with the universal guidelines for the Eucharistic liturgy. It would be helpful to read paragraphs 46 through 90 as background material on the structure of the liturgy. In the *Gather Faithfully* Participant's Booklet on pages 21–22, the section titled "Frequently Asked Questions for Serving as an Extraordinary Minister of Holy Communion" was adapted from *General Instruction on the Roman Missal* and represents the universal norms. However, not all questions can be answered because much depends on the configuration of the local space and the local norms. In order to fully prepare for this session, please review the questions found in step four of this session. Confer with your priest in finding the answers to the questions.

Session Activity

Opening Prayer

Gather the participants around a candle. Select a leader and a reader from among the participants and give one participant the matches or lighter. Ask the reader to prepare to proclaim Matthew 26:26–30.

Leader: We have arrived physically. Now let's take a moment to arrive in our hearts and spirits as well. (Allow for a few moments of silence.)

Leader: As a reminder that we, though many, are one Body with Jesus Christ, we will light the candle and begin. (At this point, the participant with the matches or lighter may light the candle.)

Leader: Let's begin together, in the name of the Father, and of the Son, and of the Holy Spirit.

Reading: Matthew 26:26–30 (from page 19 in the *Gather Faithfully* Participant's Booklet).

Leader: Father, your son Jesus is our bread of life and our cup of salvation. Be with us as we prepare to be ministers of this most Holy Sacrament. We trust in your grace to make us ready. We make this prayer through Jesus Christ our LORD. Amen.

Activity

1. Gather the participants in the community's worship space and invite them to turn to the "Prayer of Abandonment" from session 2, on page 18 in the *Gather Faithfully* Participant's Booklet. Invite the participants to take a few quiet moments to review the "Prayer of Abandonment" and recall the last session. Ask a participant to pray the "Prayer of Abandonment" aloud after a few moments of silence.

2. After this time of recollection, invite the participants to turn to the sections titled "Introduction" and "The Rites of the Eucharistic Liturgy," on pages 19 and 20–21 in the *Gather Faithfully* Participant's Booklet. Please read the content of these sections with them. The intention is to have the participants become familiar with the movement of the liturgy. We want them to have confidence. Part of this confidence will come with familiarity with the liturgy.

3. After becoming familiar with the rites of the liturgy of the Eucharist and with the Communion rite in particular, review "Frequently Asked Questions for Serving as an Extraordinary Minister of Holy Communion," on pages 21–22 in the *Gather Faithfully* Participant's Booklet. Follow the instructions and practice with the participants. Allow them to use the sacred vessels in order for them to become comfortable with them. Also allow the participants to make notes in

their Participant Booklets. Many different worship spaces require different or unique ways of following the instructions. It will be important to allow the participants to have every opportunity to become comfortable with their movement.

4. As the leader, try to think through other policies and procedures and review them with the participants:

- Will there be a sign-in procedure before the liturgy?
- Will they receive a Communion station assignment, or will they be expected to know where the stations are, and fill them in as they leave the sanctuary?
- Do they enter the sanctuary together or one by one?
- Where do they stand when they approach the altar?
- Who will bring them Communion?
- Will they receive Communion under both forms?
- How will they receive their Communion vessels?
- Will they carry their Communion vessel in one hand or two?
- Do they wait until everyone has received their Communion vessels, or do they leave for their station as soon as they have received their vessel?
- What will the minister do if he or she runs out of bread or wine?
- What if their Communion station is finished, but other stations are still distributing Communion?
- Do the ministers assist with purification of the vessels or in consuming any consecrated wine that is left?
- If the ministers return their vessels to the sanctuary, how do they leave the sanctuary?
- Do they return to their pews? Will they carry the Communion vessels to the sacristy or to the Adoration chapel?

Knowledge builds confidence. If the young people are confident that they know what to do, they will be confident in how they do it.

5. To conclude this session, invite the participants to gather around the altar and to stand with their hands extended as though receiving Communion in the hands. Invite them to close their eyes.

- When we come to Communion, we bring all that we are. In your mind now, place those things in your hands that are uppermost in your mind . . . your joys, concerns, hopes, fears. . . .

- And when Jesus meets us in this most Holy Sacrament, he brings who he is. Imagine now that he stands before you. He sees those things in your hands as your five loaves and two fish. He would like you to give them to him so that he can bless them, and use them to feed the multitude. If you would like to give what is in your hand to Jesus, do so now in the quietness of your heart.

After a moment of silence, ask the participants to turn to "The Grail Prayer," on page 23 in the *Gather Faithfully* Participant's Booklet. Invite them to pray it aloud together:

> LORD Jesus,
> I give you my hands to do your work.
> I give you my feet to go your way.
> I give you my eyes to see as you do.
> I give you my tongue to speak your words.
> I give you my mind that you may think in me.
> I give you my spirit that you may pray in me.
> Above all, I give you my heart that you may love in me your Father
>   and all humanity.
> I give you my whole self that you may grow in me, so that it is you,
> LORD Jesus, who live and work and pray in me.
> Amen.
>
> (Nicholas Hutchinson, *Walk in My Presence*)

Ministry of Altar Server

Session 1

Overview

Session Goal

- To learn that serving as a minister of the altar server is a ministry both in the Eucharistic liturgy and in all aspects of life

Materials

- ❑ a candle
- ❑ matches or a lighter
- ❑ *Gather Faithfully* Participant's Booklet
- ❑ pens or pencils, one for each participant
- ❑ newsprint
- ❑ markers
- ❑ masking tape
- ❑ roses and lilies, six of each placed where the participants cannot see or smell them

Session Activity

Opening Prayer

Gather the participants around a candle. Select a leader and a reader from among the participants and give one participant the matches or lighter. Ask the reader to prepare to proclaim Philippians 2:1–11.

Leader: We have arrived physically. Now let's take a moment to arrive in our hearts and spirits as well. (Allow for a few moments of silence.)

Leader: As a reminder that we, like Jesus, are called to be servants, we will light the candle and begin. (At this point, the participant with the matches or lighter may light the candle.)

Leader: Let's begin together, in the name of the Father, and of the Son, and of the Holy Spirit.

Reading: Philippians 2:1–11 (from pages 24–25 in the *Gather Faithfully* Participant's Booklet).

Leader: Father, although your son Jesus was fully God, he became fully human. He left his ruling throne and became a servant. Give us the grace we need to follow his example. Help us to serve as Jesus served by letting our lives and ministry be a way people encounter your grace. We make this prayer through Jesus Christ our LORD. Amen.

Activity

1. Ask the young people to turn to the reading titled "The Altar Server's True Light," on page 25 in the *Gather Faithfully* Participant's Booklet. Invite a participant to read this section aloud of a general audience by Pope John Paul II in which he addresses lay ministers of the altar. After the reading make the following or similar comments:

- In this address to altar servers, Pope John Paul II is encouraging altar servers not to leave their ministry at the liturgy. Rather, the light that they carry in the liturgy should continue to shine for their friends, family, and even strangers.

2. After these remarks, refer the participants to "Living the Good Life," on pages 25–26 in the *Gather Faithfully* Participant's Booklet, and ask them to complete the exercise under that section. While the young people are writing, set up a few areas with a piece of newsprint and four markers. Have enough "stations" to allow the participants to work in groups of four or five.

3. After the participants have had time to write and you have set up the stations with the newsprint and markers, invite the young people to gather around a piece of newsprint in groups of four or five. Ask them to describe the people they wrote about to the other members of the group. As they do so, the other group members use the markers to write on the newsprint the things that they hear the group member saying. It is okay for an answer to be repeated by group members.

4. When the groups have finished discussing, have them hang their newsprint on the wall and have the participants make their way around the room reading the qualities that have been identified. Then lead a discussion with these or similar questions:

- What are some of the qualities that you see listed?

- Why do you think that these qualities make a difference?

As the young people continue the discussion, take the opportunity to ensure that the following points are included:

- Action is a powerful means to carry a message. We are able to tell what a person thinks or feels by how they act.
- Faith is communicated as much with our example as it is with our words.

5. After the discussion, ask the young people to sit in a circle, and instruct them to close their eyes. Tell them that you are going to place items around the circle. They are to identify the items without opening their eyes. At this point, walk around the circle with the roses, then the lilies, and then ask the young people to identify the items. Use this experience to emphasize the following:

- The impression that you and I leave is like an aroma. Take a look at the pieces of newsprint on the wall. The people described have left lasting impressions with you. . . . Their aroma has stayed with you so much that they are the first thing you think of when asked to describe a person of faith. What kind of impression, what aroma, do you want to leave people with? Are they some of the things listed on the newsprint? Think about how you described your person or person of faith to the group. How would you like to be described? What would you like your reputation to be? Please turn to "Who Do I Want to Be?" on page 26 in the *Gather Faithfully* Participant's Booklet, and write your answers to the questions.

If time allows, gather the participants in groups of four to five and invite them to share what they have written in their booklets with one another. Otherwise, move to the closing prayer.

6. Ask the young people to bring their Participant's Booklet and gather in a circle around the candle. Invite them to select two faith-filled qualities they want to embody. Encourage them to voice these qualities as their prayer.

When all have had the opportunity to share, conclude with the following prayer:

LORD, hear and receive us this day. You left your ruling throne in heaven to come to us. Help us now. Help the best part of us rise up and become servant kings and servant queens in your heavenly Reign. We make this prayer through Christ our LORD. Amen.

Ministry of Altar Server

Session 2

Overview

Session Goals

- To have the participants understand the concept of Christian dignity
- To familiarize the participants with the alb or the cassock and surplice to be worn when ministering as an altar server

Materials

- ❑ a candle
- ❑ matches or a lighter
- ❑ *Gather Faithfully* Participant's Booklet
- ❑ pens or pencils, one for each participant
- ❑ the attire worn by altar servers in your community (alb or cassock and surplice)
- ❑ a piece of white ribbon at least two inches wide and five feet long, one for each young person, placed out of sight

Session Activity

Opening Prayer

Gather the participants around a candle. Select a leader and a reader from among the participants and give one participant the matches or lighter. Ask the reader to prepare to proclaim Galatians 3:27–29.

Leader: We have arrived physically. Now let's take a moment to arrive in our hearts and spirits as well. (Allow for a few moments of silence.)

Leader: As a reminder that we, like Jesus, are called to be servants, we will light the candle and begin. (At this point, the participant with the matches or lighter may light the candle.)

Leader: Let's begin together, in the name of the Father, and of the Son, and of the Holy Spirit.

Reading: Galatians 3:27–29 (from page 26 in the *Gather Faithfully* Participant's Booklet).

Leader: Father, we have been baptized in the name of your son Jesus Christ. We who were dead have now been raised to new life. May our lives be living examples of the abundant life that is found in an intimate relationship with Jesus Christ. We make this prayer through the same Jesus Christ our LORD. Amen.

Activity

1. Instruct the participants to turn to page 26 in the *Gather Faithfully* Participant's Booklet. Have them complete the section titled "Christian Dignity" and let them know they will be encouraged to share their answers with others. After allowing time for them to write, divide the participants into groups of five or six and ask them to share their responses with one another.

2. After allowing several moments for the small-group discussion, gather the participants for a large-group discussion. Step through the questions one by one and ask for volunteers to respond. Be certain the discussion includes the following:

- Dignity is not practiced very much in our culture. Humor can be based on making fun of an individual or group. People are put down so others can look better. People are often used as a means to get something. We can fail to treat people with the dignity they deserve. Perhaps we even put ourselves down before someone does it for us.

- To understand what it is to be a server, dignity must also be understood. The server must act and respond with dignity and must treat others with dignity. This giving and receiving of dignity is a message to the congregation. When a server carries out the task of serving with dignity, it reminds the parish community that this is a holy task, a sacred task.

3. Invite the participants to turn to page 28 in the *Gather Faithfully* Participant's Booklet. Have them complete the section titled "The White Cloth." Give them a few moments to write. The following answers may emerge:

- *First Communion.* Many communities have the tradition of wearing white.
- *Matrimony.* Brides traditionally wear white gowns.
- *A Funeral.* A white pall or cloth is placed on the casket.
- *The Eucharist.* The priest, deacon, and other ministers wear albs.

After allowing the participants time to write, make the following or similar comments:

○ The garment we were given at Baptism follows us through many of the most important moments of our lives. This "outward sign of your Christian dignity" is as a reminder of a very real truth: you are a son or daughter of God, and you have a holy dignity.

4. After your comments on dignity, gather the participants around the altar.

○ Outside of the liturgy, we treat people with dignity because they are made in the image of God and are holy. Within this worship space, we are most clearly seen as what we really are: images of God. As altar servers you will wear the outside sign of your dignity as a Christian. The alb or cassock and surplice you wear reminds you, and the entire community, of the Baptism we share and the sign of our Christian dignity, which all have been given.

○ As servers, we begin from the moment we enter the church. When we bow or genuflect, we must do so with dignity. Let's bow together to the altar and acknowledge it as a consecrated symbol of Christ (bow) and again (bow). Let us approach the tabernacle and genuflect reverence to the Blessed Sacrament (genuflect) and again (genuflect).

At this point, invite the young people to put on the servers' vestments. Ensure that each young person tries on a vestment. Be familiar with and explain where the vestments are stored and anything they need to know about wearing them.

5. After allowing time for the participants to put on their vestments, gather them around the altar. Invite them to bow or genuflect as they draw near. As they gather around the altar, get the white ribbons from where you have placed them. Tell them that as a reminder of the dignity they were given at Baptism, you will place a ribbon around their neck. As you do, invite the rest of the group to say the words from the baptismal rite from *The Rites of the Catholic Church* in unison. "_____, [insert name] see in this white garment the outward sign of your Christian dignity."

Once all have received the white ribbons, pray:

> LORD of whatever is true, whatever is holy, though it is sometimes hard to believe in our dignity, we believe that your word is true. Help us to be givers and receivers of dignity. May all we do, within this church and when we leave, give glory to your most holy name. We make this prayer in the name of Jesus Christ, in whose name we have all been baptized. Amen.

Ministry of Altar Server

Session 3

Overview

Session Goals

- To familiarize the participants with the order of the Eucharistic liturgy
- To practice serving the needs of the particular worshiping community

Materials

- ❑ a candle
- ❑ matches or a lighter
- ❑ *Gather Faithfully* Participant's Booklet
- ❑ pens or pencils, one for each participants
- ❑ a copy of the *Sacramentary*
- ❑ liturgical symbols and objects, e.g., processional cross, candles, and a thurible

Trainer's Preparation

General Instruction on the Roman Missal provides the Church with the universal guidelines for the Eucharistic liturgy. It could be helpful to read paragraphs 46 through 90 as background material on the structure of the liturgy. In the *Gather Faithfully* Participant's Booklet on pages 30–33, the section titled "Being a Servant During the Eucharistic Liturgy" provides an overview of the *General Instruction on the Roman Missal,* paragraphs 120 through 170 and paragraphs 187 through 193, "The Duties of the Acolyte." However, not all questions can be answered because much depends on the configuration of the local space and the local norms. Confer with your priest in finding the answers to any remaining questions.

Session Activity

Opening Prayer

Gather the participants around a candle. Select a leader and a reader from among the participants and give one participant the matches or lighter. Ask the reader to prepare to proclaim Luke 10:38–42.

Leader: We have arrived physically. Now let's take a moment to arrive in our hearts and spirits as well. (Allow for a few moments of silence.)

Leader: As a reminder that we, like Jesus, are called to be servants, we will light the candle and begin. (At this point, the participant with the matches or lighter may light the candle.)

Leader: Let's begin together, in the name of the Father, and of the Son, and of the Holy Spirit.

Reading: Luke 10:38–42 (from page 28 in the *Gather Faithfully* Participant's Booklet).

Leader: LORD of love, receive our ministry as a sign of our love for you. It is easy, LORD, to be worried and anxious about the many things of this ministry, but help us choose the better part. We make this prayer through Jesus Christ our LORD. Amen.

Activity

1. Explain to the young people that this is a hands-on session. Ask them to bring the Participant's Booklet and enter the community's worship space. Encourage them to use what was learned in session two regarding bowing and genuflecting.

Gather the participants in the front of the room and invite them to turn to "Order of the Liturgy," on pages 29–30 in the *Gather Faithfully* Participant's Booklet. Read through the parts of the Eucharistic liturgy with the participants. Based on your preparation with the *General Instruction on the Roman Missal,* be prepared to answer any questions. In going over the parts of the liturgy, the participants should achieve a level of knowledge that will help them serve with confidence.

2. After seeing the parts, give the participants insight in to the larger picture. Relay the following information to the participants:

   ○ The ministry of altar server can be compared to a server at an elegant restaurant. The server is not noticed, but everything gets taken care of.

   ○ Don't be afraid of making a mistake. Be confident. Everyone makes mistakes. This is one reason why we work as a team. If I forget something, you can remind me. Most times, the mistake is only known by you, the other servers, and the priest.

3. After these remarks, go through the Eucharistic liturgy moment by moment as seen in the *General Instruction on the Roman Missal* paragraph numbers 120 through 170 and paragraphs 187 through 193, "The Duties of the Acolyte." If your community celebrates the Eucharistic liturgy with both a priest and a deacon, paragraphs 171 through 186 are also applicable. Encourage the participants to make notes in their *Gather Faithfully* Participant's Booklet. Take your time and allow for the participants to ask clarifying questions.

4. After allowing time to practice and for questions, conclude by gathering the participants together in a circle and asking the participants to place their hands on the shoulders of the person on either side of them and close their eyes. Then pray:

> Holy Spirit, be with us now. Teach us how to pray. Bless us and give us what we need for this ministry, in this building and as we go into the world. Living God, you are always present among us through your Holy Spirit. Your Son comes to us at this place in the most holy Eucharist. Let us be carriers of your Good News as we go into the world. Make us servants at this table, and of all humankind. We make this prayer in the name of Jesus our LORD. Amen.

Ministry of Hospitality

Session 1

Overview

Session Goals

- To help the participants recall the feelings of being welcomed and unwelcomed
- To help participants understand that from the moment a person enters the liturgy they can do much to ensure that the stranger is welcomed as a family member

Materials

- ❑ a candle
- ❑ matches or a lighter
- ❑ *Gather Faithfully* Participant's Booklet
- ❑ newsprint
- ❑ markers, two or three for each participant
- ❑ pens or pencils, one for each participant
- ❑ paper

Session Activity

Opening Prayer

Gather the participants around a candle. Select a leader and a reader from among the participants and give one participant the matches or lighter. Ask the reader to prepare to proclaim Matthew 25:34–40.

Leader: We have arrived physically. Now let's take a moment to arrive in our hearts and spirits as well. (Allow for a few moments of silence.)

Leader: As a reminder that Jesus has given us a light to shine, we will light the candle and begin. (At this point, the participant with the matches or lighter may light the candle.)

Leader: Let's begin together, in the name of the Father, and of the Son, and of the Holy Spirit.

Reading: Matthew 25:34–40 (from page 34 in the *Gather Faithfully* Participant's Booklet).

Leader: O LORD our God and Father of all, through your son Jesus Christ we are drawn together as one family. Open our hearts to receive one another as you receive us all. We make this prayer through Jesus Christ our LORD. Amen.

Activity

1. Gather the young people in groups of five or six and give each group a page of newsprint and markers. Ask the participants to recall a time when they entered a room or situation as a stranger and instruct them in the following manner:

- Draw a line through the middle of the newsprint and create two separate halves.

- Write on the newsprint what feelings you had when you entered the room as a stranger on one half of the newsprint, leaving the other half blank.

2. After allowing the participants a few moments to answer, ask them to think about going to the house of a person whom they love to visit or to recall a time they were treated as though they were the most important person in the world.

- Write on the newsprint what feelings you had or have when entering this home.

After allowing a time for them to write, invite the participants to share with the other group members their reflections recorded on both sides of the newsprint.

3. Starting with side one, facilitate a large-group discussion. Keep track of the answers on two separate pieces of newsprint and hang them on the wall following each discussion. The following questions may facilitate the discussion:

- Have you ever had the experience of walking into a room and having everyone stop talking and look at you? What was that like?

- Have you ever walked into a room and wondered where you would sit or stand or to whom you would talk?

- Have you ever regretted going somewhere because no one spoke to you?

After allowing an appropriate amount of time for side one, move on to side two. The following questions may facilitate the discussion:

- What makes you feel welcomed somewhere?

- Have you ever been reluctant to go somewhere, but enjoyed yourself once you arrived? What made you enjoy it?

4. Invite the participants to read over the newsprint and invite them to turn to and complete the section titled "Who Is the Stranger?" on pages 34–35 in the *Gather Faithfully* Participant's Booklet.

After allowing a few moments to answer, invite the participants to discuss their responses and include the following points:

- This person is a member of the family of God, and is your brother or sister in Christ.

- This person is a member of the community. Though she or he may feel isolated and alone, this person belongs here, as a member of the Body of Christ.

5. Refer the participants to the opening scriptural reading, Matthew 25:34–40, on page 34 in the *Gather Faithfully* Participant's Booklet. Ask them to reread the passage silently and then answer the question under the section titled "I Was a Stranger," on page 35 in the *Gather Faithfully* Participant's Booklet. Invite them to share their reflections with their small group.

6. Refer the participants back to the person walking into Mass. Under the section titled "You Welcomed Me," ask the participants to write two things the person will need in order to feel welcomed, loved, and at home.

7. To conclude, remind the participants that they have recalled experiences where they have felt both unwelcomed and welcomed. Reflecting on Jesus's call to welcome the stranger, we need to make the people we worship with feel at home.

Ask the young people to gather in a circle around the candle and conclude with the following prayer:

LORD our God and Father of all, help us to be your hands and your welcoming voice to all who enter our parish. May everyone who gathers here for prayer know of your deep abiding love for them. We make this prayer through Christ our LORD. Amen.

Note to leader: To prepare for session 2, type the young people's responses, and have copies ready for distribution. Name the document "You Welcomed Me." To prepare for session 3, save the two summary pieces of newsprint.

Ministry of Hospitality

Session 2

Overview

Session Goals

- To raise the participants' awareness that they have the capacity to make a difference in the lives of the people who enter the church
- To discover the manner in which the participants can authentically serve as ministers of hospitality

Materials

- ❑ a candle
- ❑ matches or a lighter
- ❑ *Gather Faithfully* Participant's Booklet
- ❑ pens or pencils, one for each participant
- ❑ a writing surface visible to the large group
- ❑ four bibles

Trainer's Preparation

General Instruction for the Roman Missal does not provide guidelines for ministries of hospitality. In order to create a guide for such ministers in your local community, refer to the section titled "The 'Must-Knows' and 'Must-Dos'," on pages 37–38 in the *Gather Faithfully* Participant's Booklet. You will find the following series of things that a minister of hospitality must know in order to minister. In preparation for this session, please review this list and create a guide for being a minister of hospitality in your community based on the list. Be prepared to instruct the participants based on this guide. You should know the following things:

- The location of the hymnals or worship aids
- The location of the bathrooms
- The location of the cry room
- The location of the first-aid kits
- The location reserved for those in wheelchairs
- The times for other liturgies

You should do the following things:

- Notify extraordinary ministers of Holy Communion of anyone who may need Communion brought to them
- Assist latecomers with finding a seat
- Assist the hearing impaired (if available)
- Register new parishioners
- Inform parishioners about upcoming events by referring to the parish or school bulletin

Session Activity

Opening Prayer

Gather the participants around a candle. Select a leader and a reader from among the participants and give one participant the matches or lighter. Ask the reader to prepare to proclaim Hebrews 13:1–2.

Leader: We have arrived physically. Now let's take a moment to arrive in our hearts and spirits as well. (Allow for a few moments of silence.)

Leader: As a reminder that Jesus has given us a light to shine, we will light the candle and begin. (At this point, the participant with the matches or lighter may light the candle.)

Leader: Let's begin together, in the name of the Father, and of the Son, and of the Holy Spirit.

Reading: Hebrews 13:1–2 (from page 36 in the *Gather Faithfully* Participant's Booklet).

Leader: This is called the "Prayer for Christian Unity." May it help us remember that every person who worships with us is our brother or sister in Christ:

> LORD Jesus Christ, at your Last Supper, you prayed to the Father that all should be one. Send your Holy Spirit upon all who hear your name and seek to serve you. Strengthen our faith in you, and lead us to love one another in humility. May we who have been born in one Baptism be united in one faith under one Shepherd. Amen.
>
> (James D. Watkins, comp.; *Manual of Prayers*; page 304)

Activity

1. Refer the participants to the reflections they wrote under the section titled "You Welcomed Me," on page 35 in the *Gather Faithfully* Participant's Booklet, and review the points from session 1. Ask the participants to voice the ideas they had from the reflection then write them in a place that is visible to the large group.

2. After recording their reflections, divide the participants into four groups and instruct the participants to turn to the section titled "Meet-and-Greet Bible Style," on page 36 in the *Gather Faithfully* Participant's Booklet. Give each group a Bible and assign one of the following Scripture passages to each group:

- Mark 8:1–8
- John 2:1–11
- Luke 10:38–42
- Matthew 9:9–13

Each group is to read the passage and answer the question, "What lessons are there to be learned from these Scripture passages about serving as a minister of hospitality?"

Allow some time for the groups to discuss their passages and have each group present their responses to the large group. Record these responses in a place visible to the large group.

3. Invite the participants to turn to the section titled "Meet-and-Greet My Style," on page 37 in the *Gather Faithfully* Participant's Booklet. Address the participants in the following manner and invite them to record their reflections:

- Through the ministry of hospitality, community building begins as worshipers enter our doors. By following the example of Jesus, and through our actions reminding those who enter that they belong in this family of God, we create a homecoming of sorts. In the same way we relax and feel comfortable in our grandmother's house, so too we want people to relax and be at home in the Eucharistic liturgy in the Body of Christ.

- Being a member of the Body of Christ is about building authentic relationships with each other and with the LORD. Authentic relationships require us to be real. How can you be real as a minister of hospitality? Take some time for reflection and complete the section titled, "Meet-and-Greet My Style."

Invite the participants to form groups of four or five and ask the participants to share their reflections with others in the group.

4. After allowing a chance for discussion, ask the participants to turn to the section titled "The 'Must-Knows' and 'Must-Dos'," on pages 37–38 in the *Gather Faithfully* Participant's Booklet. Please refer to the guide you created during your preparation and review this section with the participants. Invite them to make notes about the particular way your community celebrates the liturgy.

5. To conclude, gather the participants in a circle around the candle and invite them to turn to the "Prayer for Christian Unity," on page 38 in the *Gather Faithfully* Participant's Booklet. Pray the prayer in unison.

Ministry of Hospitality

Session 3

Overview

Session Goals

- To develop a mission statement and prayer for the ministry of hospitality
- To learn the particular manner in which to serve as a minister of hospitality in the worshiping community

Materials

- ❑ a candle
- ❑ matches or a lighter
- ❑ *Gather Faithfully* Participant's Booklet
- ❑ pens or pencils, one for each participant
- ❑ newsprint from session 1
- ❑ blank newsprint
- ❑ markers, one for each participant

Trainer's Preparation

General Instruction for the Roman Missal does not provide guidelines for ministries of hospitality. In order to create a guide for such ministers in your local community, refer to the questions in the section titled "Checklist for Ministers of Hospitality," on pages 39–40 in the *Gather Faithfully* Participant's Booklet. In preparation for this session, please review these questions and create a guide for being a minister of hospitality in your community. Be prepared to instruct the participants based on this guide:

- Will hospitality ministers gather before Mass to pray together? If so, where?
- How will hospitality ministers learn about the day's events so that they can be prepared to answer questions?
- What entrances to the community's worship space will need to be covered?
- Will we place any ministers within the worship space to help people find seats?
- Will we wear nametags?

- Are there other steps we can take in this space to create a welcoming atmosphere?
- Where are the bathrooms?
- What are the handicapped accessibility options?
- What provisions are there for the hearing impaired?
- Are there problem areas in this building for people who have physical disabilities?
- Where are the cry rooms?
- If I would like to get a message to my priest, how do I do so?
- If I need to speak with an extraordinary minister of Holy Communion, how do I do so?
- What will need to be distributed at the door as worshipers arrive?
- What will need to be distributed after Mass?
- Will I have any responsibilities during Mass, such as assisting with the collection?

Session Activity

Opening Prayer

Gather the participants around a candle. Select a leader and a reader from among the participants and give one participant the matches or lighter. Ask the reader to prepare to proclaim Matthew 5:13–16.

Leader: We have arrived physically. Now let's take a moment to arrive in our hearts and spirits as well. (Allow for a few moments of silence.)

Leader: As a reminder that Jesus has given us a light to shine, we will light the candle and begin. (At this point, the participant with the matches or lighter may light the candle.)

Leader: Let's begin together, in the name of the Father, and of the Son, and of the Holy Spirit.

Reading: Matthew 5:13–16 (from page 38 in the *Gather Faithfully* Participant's Booklet).

Leader: O Lord of every nation, you have given each of us a light to shine before your people. Use our light, we pray, to draw people to you. May all who encounter our light encounter in us the person of your Son Christ Jesus. We make this prayer through Christ our Lord. Amen.

Activity

1. Lay out the pieces of newsprint from session 1. Then lay out blank newsprint and give each participant a marker. Invite the young people to review the responses on the newsprint from session 1, and their reflections from sessions 1 and 2 recorded in their *Gather Faithfully* Participant's Booklet.

2. Inform the participants that they will write a mission statement and prayer for their ministry of hospitality. After they have reviewed the information in their Participant's Booklet and on the newsprint, ask the participants to write words or phrases on the blank pieces of newsprint that are particularly meaningful about the ministry of hospitality.

3. After allowing time for the participants to identify their phrases, propose a mission statement that you feel captures their sentiments. Present this to the group and allow for their input until a consensus is reached on the statement. Once the participants agree on the mission statement, have a volunteer write it on a clean piece of newsprint, and hang it up. Invite the participants to write the mission statement in their Participant's Booklet. Similar to the process by which the mission statement was written, ask the group to write a prayer that expresses their hopes for their ministry of hospitality. Instruct the participants to write their prayer in the section titled "Minister's Prayer" on page 39.

4. If you have not already assembled there, go to the community's worship space and gather at the front. Using the checklist provided on pages 39–40 in the *Gather Faithfully* Participant's Booklet, lead the participants through the guide you created in preparing for this session.

5. When everyone is comfortable with their ministry, ask the participants to gather in a circle around the candle. Invite the young people to turn to the prayer written by the group in "Minister's Prayer," on page 39 in the *Gather Faithfully* Participant's Booklet. Ask them to say the prayer in unison.

Ministry of Sacristan

Session 1

Overview

Session Goals

- To understand a sense of the sacred
- To understand the importance of the often hidden ministry of sacristan

Materials

- ❑ a candle
- ❑ matches or a lighter
- ❑ *Gather Faithfully* Participant's Booklet
- ❑ pens or pencils, one for each participant
- ❑ holy cards of the Last Supper, one for each participant

Session Activity

Opening Prayer

Gather the participants around a candle. Select a leader and a reader from among the participants and give one participant the matches or lighter. Ask the reader to prepare to proclaim Matthew 5:13–16 and 1 Corinthians 11:23–26.

Leader: We have arrived physically. Now let's take a moment to arrive in our hearts and spirits as well. (Allow for a few moments of silence.)

Leader: As a reminder that the Jesus Christ is the light of the world, we will light the candle and begin. (At this point, the participant with the matches or lighter may light the candle.)

Leader: Let's begin together, in the name of the Father, and of the Son, and of the Holy Spirit.

Leader: Jesus, you are the light of the world.

Reading: Matthew 5:13–16 (from page 41 in the *Gather Faithfully* Participant's Booklet) and 1 Corinthians 11:23–26 from page 71 of this book.

Leader: O good and gracious Father, teach us to let our light shine so that all might come to find you. We ask this through your Son, our LORD Jesus Christ. Amen.

Activity

1. Gather with the participants outside of the community's worship space. Tell the young people that in a moment you are going to take them into the worship space. Once you arrive, you would like them to spread out and write down one-word answers to the question posed in the section titled "Our Place," on page 41 in the *Gather Faithfully* Participant's Booklet. Challenge the participants to not stop after a couple of minutes; they should keep looking and thinking. Invite them to walk around freely, yet silently, and look at things more closely than usual.

At this point, lead them to the church.

2. After allowing about 10 minutes, invite the young people back together. Ask them to share some of their words. Work with their observations. What they see will remind them of different aspects of their faith. Be certain to include the following points in the discussion:

○ This space is designed to lift our eyes toward God and toward the things of God.

○ This space is holy and sacred. You are holy and sacred.

○ In the role of sacristan, you will be in charge of sacred things and near sacred people. When you respond to that by treating them with reverence, it reminds the congregation that they are in a sacred place, that the liturgy is a sacred work.

3. Divide the group into smaller groups of three or four and ask the participants to turn to the section titled "Mary Treasured in Her Heart," on page 42 in the *Gather Faithfully* Participant's Booklet. Instruct them to read the passage carefully and to complete the questions as instructed. When they have finished writing, allow time for them to share their responses with the other members of the small group.

4. After allowing time for discussion in the small groups, ask for the participants' responses in a large-group discussion. Incorporate the following into your discussion:

○ We are often too accustomed to liturgy and do not respond with the awe and the reverence that the shepherds did.

○ Sometimes we are simply unaware that the sacred is among us.

○ There are things in life that we experience that go beyond words. Because they are hard to describe, you, like Mary, treasure them in your heart.

○ As a sacristan, much of your work will be hidden. In fact, you will most be noticed if you forget something. Yet, your role, like that of the shepherds and Mary, will also bring you close to something glorious, something beautiful, something sacred. Your work will both prepare the community for the invitation to encounter Jesus and will aid us as we experience him.

5. To conclude, gather the young people together in a circle around the altar and distribute the holy cards of the Last Supper. Explain to the young people that what happens at the liturgy is as real as the Last Supper. In fact, we join the Last Supper and we become part of the scene that we are looking at.

Leave a few moments of silence.

Reading: 1 Corinthians 11:23–26

> For I received from the LORD what I also handed on to you, that the LORD Jesus on the night when he was betrayed took a loaf of bread, and when he had given thanks, he broke it and said, "This is my body that is for you. Do this in remembrance of me." In the same way he took the cup also, after supper, saying, "This cup is the new covenant in my blood. Do this, as often as you drink it, in remembrance of me." For as often as you eat this bread and drink the cup, you proclaim the LORD's death until he comes.

Leader: O Jesus of the Sacrament most holy, give us the grace to see the sacred in the ordinary. May whatever we do, in speech or in action, give you glory. Amen.

Ministry of Sacristan

Session 2

Overview

Session Goals

- To learn how to use the ordo in order to prepare the liturgical books for the Eucharistic liturgy
- To learn the basic vocabulary needed by sacristans

Materials

- ❏ a candle
- ❏ matches or a lighter
- ❏ *Gather Faithfully* Participant's Booklet
- ❏ pens or pencils, one for each participant
- ❏ several copies of each of the liturgical books: the *Sacramentary*, the *Lectionary*, and the ordo
- ❏ dates of upcoming Sundays or all-school liturgies, written on small pieces of paper and placed in a small container (be sure at least one of the dates is a feast or solemnity, such as the feast of Christ the King)

Trainer's Preparation

It will be important to familiarize yourself with the ordo, the *Lectionary*, and the *Sacramentary*. The ordo is a small book that is printed annually. It guides a community through the liturgical year by indicating which feasts will be celebrated at the liturgy and which readings should be read on a certain day. The *Lectionary* contains the biblical readings used at the liturgy, and the *Sacramentary* contains the prayers used at the Eucharistic liturgy.

First, turn to the ordo and select a day of your choosing from the calendar. On that day in the ordo, you will see a reference that reads in this or a similar manner: "In Mass readings no. 115." This number refers to a number found in the *Lectionary*. In the *Lectionary*, every set of daily readings receives a number designation. Take the sample number given, 115, and turn in the *Lectionary* to number 115. You will find that number 115 corresponds to the readings from the eighteenth Sunday of the year. In the *Sacramentary*, the opening prayer, the prayer over the Gifts, and the prayer after Communion that correspond to the eighteenth Sunday of the year are found in the section titled, "Proper of Seasons."

Also, please review the list of terms on pages 44–45 in the *Gather Faithfully* Participant's Booklet, in the section titled "Sacred Vocabulary." It will be important for you to be able to identify the following items.

alb	dalmatic
ambo	incense
chalice	presider
chasuble	purificator
concelebrant	sacrarium
corporal	stole
cruet	tabernacle

Session Activity

Opening Prayer

Gather the participants around a candle. Select a leader and a reader from among the participants and give one participant the matches or lighter. Ask the reader to prepare to proclaim Luke 7:1–10.

Leader: We have arrived physically. Now let's take a moment to arrive in our hearts and spirits as well. (Allow for a few moments of silence.)

Leader: As a reminder that Jesus is the light of the world, we will light the candle and begin. (At this point, the participant with the matches or lighter may light the candle.)

Leader: Let's begin together, in the name of the Father, and of the Son, and of the Holy Spirit.

Leader: Jesus, you love those who love your people. You call us forth to be your hands and heart.

Reading: Luke 7:1–10 (from pages 43–44 in the *Gather Faithfully* Participant's Booklet).

Leader: O kind and merciful Jesus, give us the grace to be like this centurion. He cared for people, he served them, and he brought you to them. May all we do and say in the ministry of sacristan do the same. We make this prayer in your most holy name. Amen.

Activity

1. Divide the group into smaller groups of four or five. Give each group a copy of the ordo, the *Sacramentary,* and the *Lectionary.*

Begin with the ordo. Drawing on your preparation, introduce the ordo and include the fact that the numbers correspond to numbers in the *Lectionary.* Use the previous Sunday as a reference point and demonstrate how to find the prayers from the *Sacramentary* and the readings in the *Lectionary* that correspond to the appropriate Sunday.

2. Invite the participants to reach into the small container in which the dates of upcoming Sundays or all-school liturgies have been placed. Have each group draw one of the pieces of paper and have them find the information they need in the ordo, the *Lectionary,* and the *Sacramentary.*

Check their work. Then have them draw another piece of paper and repeat.

Ask all the groups to find the information for the upcoming Sunday. Assign the following to different groups and have them read their assigned texts:

- the Collect (the opening prayer)
- the Psalm reading
- the Gospel reading
- the closing prayer

This would be a good opportunity to make a point about the universality of the Church. This Sunday these prayers and readings will be heard all over the world. The words will be spoken in English, Russian, Spanish, Japanese, Swahili, Portuguese, French, and many other languages. The following points can be made in a discussion:

- ○ By sharing common prayer, we are connected spiritually. We are, in a sense, pointed toward the same thing, praying for the same things.

- ○ The Eucharistic liturgy is never an isolated event but is intimately connected with the Eucharistic celebrations of other Catholics all over the world, past, present, and future.

3. Remind the participants of the sacredness they discovered in session 1. They are sacred and the liturgical items they will work with are sacred. Now is the time they will become more familiar with these sacred, liturgical items. Lead the participants into the community's sacristy and have them identify the items described in the section titled "Sacred Vocabulary," on pages 44–45 in the *Gather Faithfully* Participant's Booklet. Give the participants free reign of the sacristy to identify the applicable items on the list. Be sure to guide them if they do not know where to look for the all of the items.

4. After each participant has identified the items and is comfortable with the vocabulary, gather them in a circle around the altar and invite someone to read Luke 7:1–10 again. After the reading, close with this prayer:

> LORD, this centurion loved his people so much that he built a synagogue for them. Receive our work, we pray, as a sign of our love for you and your people. May we build a house of prayer together. We ask this in the name of Jesus, who is true God and true man. Amen.

Ministry of Sacristan

Session 3

Overview

Session Goals

- To learn the duties of the sacristan before, during, and after the Eucharistic liturgy
- To build comfort and confidence within the sacristans

Materials

☐ a candle

☐ matches or a lighter

☐ *Gather Faithfully* Participant's Booklet

☐ pens or pencils, one for each participant

☐ copies of the liturgical books: the *Sacramentary*, the *Lectionary*, and the ordo

Trainer's Preparation

To prepare for this session, please refer to the section titled "Sacristan's Checklist," on pages 45–49 in the *Gather Faithfully* Participant's Booklet. You will find the following topics covered therein:

ordo
the *Sacramentary*
the *Lectionary*
hymnal
miscellaneous
incense
vestments
Communion vessels and bread and wine to be consecrated
credence table
sanctuary
during Mass
purification of the vessels
after the liturgy

The session begins with the participants searching for items on the checklist. It will be important to have the location of the items identified prior to the session.

Session Activity

Opening Prayer

Gather the participants around a candle. Select a leader and a reader from among the participants and give one participant the matches or lighter. Ask the reader to prepare to proclaim Matthew 26:17–19.

Leader: We have arrived physically. Now let's take a moment to arrive in our hearts and spirits as well. (Allow for a few moments of silence.)

Leader: As a reminder that Jesus is the light of the world, we will light the candle and begin. (At this point, the participant with the matches or lighter may light the candle.)

Leader: Let's begin together, in the name of the Father, and of the Son, and of the Holy Spirit.

Leader: Jesus, hear our prayers as we gather to prepare for your Holy Mass.

Reading: Matthew 26:17–19 (from page 45 in the *Gather Faithfully* Participant's Booklet).

Leader: Jesus, you can do all things. You need nothing from us, but you invite us to participate in the preparing of the meal. We thank you for this great privilege, and we pray that you will find in us a worthy servant. We make this prayer in your most holy name. Amen.

Activity

1. Ask the young people to turn to the section titled "Sacristan's Checklist," on pages 45–49 in the *Gather Faithfully* Participant's Booklet. Begin by reviewing where to find the items on the checklist.

2. After the review, walk through and practice everything for the preparation for the upcoming Sunday liturgy or the next school-wide liturgy. As a guide for the walk-through, a section titled "Order of the Liturgy" has been included on pages 49–51 in the *Gather Faithfully* Participant's Booklet. Space has been provided to allow the participants to take notes.

Make a complete "dress rehearsal" by lighting the incense and pouring the wine. Of course, the sacred elements will not be consecrated. Nonetheless, it will provide an opportunity for the sacristans to become comfortable with the sacred elements and to build confidence.

If it would be helpful, choose another feast day and practice again.

3. To conclude, gather in a circle around the altar.

Reading: Proclaim Matthew 26:17–19 again from page 45 in the *Gather Faithfully* Participant's Booklet.

Leader: Ask everyone to place their hands on the shoulders of the people on either side of them?

LORD, we have prepared your table. We long to be with you at the meal. Help us, LORD, to be a reflection of your Apostles who served you at the Last Supper.

I invite you now to pray quietly in your heart for the person on your right. Ask God to bless, and prepare him or her for the ministry of sacristan. (Allow a few moments of silence.)

Pray now for the person on your left.

Hear and receive our prayers, LORD, for we bring them to you, confident that you will answer our needs. We make this prayer in the most holy name of Jesus. Amen.

Ministry of Cantor

Session 1

Overview

Session Goals

- To introduce the nature of the Book of Psalms
- To introduce the uniqueness of the Psalms in the liturgy

Materials

- ☐ a candle

- ☐ matches or a lighter

- ☐ *Gather Faithfully* Participant's Booklet

- ☐ bibles, one for each participant

- ☐ pens or pencils, one for each participant

- ☐ a writing surface visible to the large group

Session Activity

Opening Prayer

Gather the participants around a candle. Select a leader and a reader from among the participants and give one participant the matches or lighter. Ask the reader to prepare to proclaim Psalm 57:7–11.

Leader: We have arrived physically. Now let's take a moment to arrive in our hearts and spirits as well. (Allow for a few moments of silence.)

Leader: As a reminder that Jesus has given us a voice that we might praise him, we will light the candle and begin. (At this point, the participant with the matches or lighter may light the candle.)

Leader: Let's begin together, in the name of the Father, and of the Son, and of the Holy Spirit.

Reading: Psalm 57:7–11 (from page 52 in the *Gather Faithfully* Participant's Booklet).

Leader: O God of glory! O LORD of all peoples! O God of faithfulness! May our souls awake to praise you. May our voices lead your people that they may acclaim your name. May we, with one voice, worship you as you deserve. We make this prayer in the name of Jesus our LORD. Amen.

Activity

1. Give a Bible to all participants and ask them to turn to the Book of Psalms. Instruct them to find the Psalm that corresponds to the day of their birth. For example if a person's birthday is April 13, that person should turn to Psalm 13. When they have found the Psalm, ask them to read it slowly to themselves.

2. After allowing a few moments, ask them to multiply their birth date by 2 and find that Psalm and read it. For example, if a person's birthday is April 13, that person should turn to Psalm 26. Finally, instruct them to pick any number between 1 and 150 and read that Psalm. Allow a few moments for the young people to do so.

3. Reading these different Psalms should supply the participants with a sampling of the emotions, themes, hopes, and concerns found in the Psalms. Ask the participants to share these with the large group. Write these reflections in a place that is visible to the large group. As part of the discussion, be sure to make the following points:

o The Psalms are prayers.

o The Psalms are the voice of someone in prayer, directed toward God; they are written in the first person, using words like, *I* and *me*, and they address God as "you."

o The Psalms deal with human experience.

o The emotions in the Psalms can engage the reader's emotions.

o The Psalms not only voice hope and joy, they voice doubt and sadness.

o The Psalms were never meant to be read, but always sung. You will often see that the first words of the Psalm are directions to the song leader—that's you!

o When you sing the Psalms, you are singing ancient words. You are singing words that the Israelites sang when they were slaves, on their great Exodus out of slavery, and after they arrived in the Promised Land. These are the words that Mary and Joseph taught Jesus to sing as he prayed with them. These words have been sung in the Eucharistic liturgy throughout the history of the Catholic Church.

4. After making these points on the Psalms, inform the young people about the Psalms' function in the Eucharistic liturgy.

o Within the Eucharistic liturgy, the Psalm becomes a singing proclamation. A reader proclaims the Old Testament and New Testament readings, the priest or deacon proclaims the Gospel. The Psalm is the only reading in which the people participate. The Psalm creates a dialogue between the people and the word of God.

o As the reader prayerfully reflects on the word to prepare for proclamation, so the cantor must also reflect on the word to be sung.

5. Invite the participants to spread around the room and ask them to turn to "Psalm *57:7–11,*" on page 52 in the *Gather Faithfully* Participant's Booklet. The participants should read the Psalm slowly three times. During the third reading ask them to underline any words or phrases that stand out. After allowing an appropriate amount of time, ask the following questions:

o What would you say is the primary feeling of the Psalmist in these verses?

o What do you think the Psalmist would like us to do?

o What attributes of God does the Psalmist bring to our attention?

o What are the ways that we, as cantors, might respond in our ministry?

6. Invite the young people to look at the words and phrases they have underlined and ask them to pick one phrase or word to focus on. Ask them to write the word or phrase under the section titled "The Holy Spirit Shines the Light," on page 53 in the *Gather Faithfully* Participant's Booklet, and to answer the questions that follow.

7. To conclude, gather together around the candle and invite the participants to turn to the words or phrases that they identified in Psalm *57:7–11.* Tell the young people that you will begin by reading the verses from Psalm *57.* Then, beginning with the person on your right, each person will read aloud the verse they have written in their participant's booklet. When all have had the opportunity to share, conclude with the following prayer:

LORD, may your word find a home in us. Give us the grace to rest with your word and to let your word rest with us. We make this prayer in the name of your son Jesus, who is the Word made flesh. Amen.

Ministry of Cantor

Session 2

Overview

Session Goals

- To understand the structure of the responsorial Psalm at the Eucharistic liturgy
- To learn the proper gesture for inviting the congregation to respond

Materials

- ❑ a candle
- ❑ matches or a lighter
- ❑ *Gather Faithfully* Participant's Booklet
- ❑ pens or pencils, one for each participant
- ❑ a music stand
- ❑ a musical setting for Psalm 23 that is familiar to the community

Session Activity

Opening Prayer

Gather the participants around a candle. Select a leader and a reader from among the participants and give one participant the matches or lighter. Ask the reader to prepare to proclaim Psalm 23.

Leader: We have arrived physically. Now let's take a moment to arrive in our hearts and spirits as well. (Allow for a few moments of silence.)

Leader: As a reminder that Jesus has given us a voice that we might praise him, we will light the candle and begin. (At this point, the participant with the matches or lighter may light the candle.)

Leader: Let's begin together, in the name of the Father, and of the Son, and of the Holy Spirit.

Reading: Psalm 23 (from page 54 in the *Gather Faithfully* Participant's Booklet).

Leader: God my shepherd, you lead me, you guide me, and with you I am confident and unafraid. May my proclamation of your words provide strength and reassurance to those who long for the Good Shepherd's touch. We make this prayer in the name of Jesus our Lord. Amen.

Activity

1. Divide the large group into groups of five or six. Ask half of the groups to study the Psalm, looking at what it reveals about who the Shepherd is and ask the other half to study the Psalm, looking at what the psalmist receives. Instruct them to record their thoughts in the section titled "Psalm 23—The Divine Shepherd," on page 54 in the *Gather Faithfully* Participant's Booklet.

2. After allowing a few moments for discussion, ask the students to think about how this Psalm might be proclaimed in song within the liturgy. Ask each group to chose a "response line," that is, which of the Psalm's verses would they choose for the congregation's part to emphasize the points they raised in their discussion? In this exercise they should do the following:

○ Choose the congregation's response

○ Choose where the stanzas, or breaks, would be

○ For those who feel comfortable, invite them to make up a melody for their response verse (it may be helpful to spread the groups out a bit so that they won't overhear each other).

3. After allowing time for them to work, ask the students to choose both a reader and a cantor. The cantor will sing the response line and the group will repeat it. If no one has put composed a melody, use the musical setting for Psalm 23 that has been prepared.

The reader will read the stanza and the response will be sung in accord with the line breaks chosen. As the reader reads, the group is listening to ensure that the reader's proclamation emphasizes either the work of the Shepherd, or what the "I" of the Psalm receives, depending on what the group has been assigned. Each group presents their Psalm to the larger group.

Allow time also to work with the gesture of invitation wherein the cantor raises his or her arm to invite the congregation to join in the singing proclamation of the word of God. When the cantor raises his or her arm in invitation to sing, he or she must use their whole arm, extended from their body, and lifted high. Lifting an arm only slightly, or a simple hand movement, sends a confusing message to the congregation. Big gestures invite big responses. The cantor in this exercise should practice a "big" gesture.

Have each group proclaim their Psalm in this manner and then discuss the experience of leading and participating in singing proclamation. The following may aid in a discussion:

- Could you observe a difference of emphasis?

- Did the musical arrangement of the response line set a tone for the group?

- What was the experience like for you when you heard other people singing "your" response line? (*Note:* The feeling of wanting the congregation to sing it correctly will come out. When we are singing other composer's music, let's remember to respect the composer's music.)

4. To conclude, ask the participants to gather in a circle around the candle, standing with the group they have been working with. Beginning with the group on your right, each cantor will step forward, and in song, proclaim their group's response line. The cantor with the invitational gesture will then invite us to join the second singing proclamation. The second group's cantor will then step forward, without waiting for direction from the leader and repeat with their group's response line. Continue until all groups have participated. Conclude with the following prayer:

Lord, today you gave us everything we needed, and so much more. We have feasted on your banquet in each other's gifts. Thank you for your gift of song that gives new life to these beautiful ancient words. We make this prayer in the name of Jesus Christ our Lord. Amen.

Ministry of Cantor

Session 3

Overview

Session Goal

- Learn the steps to the singing proclamation of the responsorial Psalm

Materials

- ❏ a candle
- ❏ matches or a lighter
- ❏ *Gather Faithfully* Participant's Booklet
- ❏ pens or pencils, one for each participant

Trainer's Preparation

To prepare for this session, review the section titled "What Motivates the Pastoral Musician?" on pages 55–56 in the *Gather Faithfully* Participant's Booklet. This paragraph from the United States Bishops' Committee on the Liturgy will give the ministerial vision.

Session Activity

Opening Prayer

Gather the participants around a candle. Select a leader and a reader from among the participants and give one participant the matches or lighter. Ask the reader to prepare to proclaim Psalm 150.

Leader: We have arrived physically. Now let's take a moment to arrive in our hearts and spirits as well. (Allow for a few moments of silence.)

Leader: As a reminder that Jesus has given us a voice that we might praise him, we will light the candle and begin. (At this point, the participant with the matches or lighter may light the candle.)

Leader: Let's begin together, in the name of the Father, and of the Son, and of the Holy Spirit.

Reading: Psalm 150 (from page 55 in the *Gather Faithfully* Participant's Booklet).

Leader: LORD of all glory, it is you who has given us the gift of song, and it is you who calls it forth from us to lead your people in worship. Help us, we pray, to be good stewards of this treasure you have given us. May the gift of our voice be a call to your people to lift their hearts and voices to you. We make this prayer through Christ our LORD. Amen.

Activity

1. Gather with the participants in the community's worship space and make sure that the sound system is on and functioning. Sit together near the front, and invite the young people to turn to the sections titled "What Motivates the Pastoral Musician?" and "Principles for the Cantor," on pages 55–56 in the *Gather Faithfully* Participant's Booklet.

Ask the participants to read through the paragraph, then lead them in a large-group discussion that includes the following points:

- A pastoral musician is one who proclaims the word of God.

- The pastoral musician is a minister not a performer. The message is important and the Psalm belongs to the entire community to proclaim.

- The pastoral musician has prayerfully reflected on the word of God, including the first and second readings, and the Gospel reading, and in so doing, identifies a theme to emphasize with the singing proclamation.

- The pastoral musician is a worshiper. She or he aids the congregation in worship.

- The pastoral musician will develop a particular style as he or she gains experience, but is always mindful that the singing proclamation is an act of worship, and that his or her efforts must enhance the Psalm, and make it easy for the congregation to join in.

- Similar to the reader, a cantor should imagine that they are Christ's spokesperson at a formal banquet. You should arrive early at the banquet, and you should be dressed for a dignified event. (Acceptable attire is usually set by local standards. While all attire should be modest, take the opportunity to instruct the participants on your community's standard for proper attire.)

- How would Christ invite others to worship? He would stand straight and project his voice clearly. His voice would fill the room. Do not think that you must only project to the microphone. Rather, think that you must invite the person in the back row to worship.

- Do not appear as though you cannot wait to get down from the ambo. As a rule of thumb, pray "Glory be to the Father, and to the Son, and to the Holy Spirit . . ." to yourself after you have finished and then step down. You want the liturgy to go at a pace that allows the word of God to soak into the congregants.

2. After reviewing these key points, it will be important to address the logistics of being a cantor in your community.

- Does the cantor wear an alb?
- Is the cantor in the procession and recession?
- Where does the cantor sit during the Mass?
- Since the Psalms are God's word, they are rightly proclaimed from the ambo, as are the other readings. Is this the custom in your community?
- When does the cantor come forward?

3. After addressing these issues, have the young people gather in the groups from session 2 and practice their refrain line again. (If they cannot remember the refrain, ask them to choose another Psalm response.) Have each individual step to the ambo while the others are spread around the worship space. At the ambo, each cantor should act as though they were serving at a Eucharistic liturgy. The cantor sings the response line, then with a big invitational gesture, invites the congregation to join the proclamation. Those in the other parts of the worship space should confirm the following:

- The cantor can be clearly heard
- The cantor looked confident and comfortable
- The inviting gesture offered a clear invitation to sing

4. After all have had a chance to practice and to become comfortable, conclude by gathering in a circle. Ask the participants to put their hands on the shoulders of the people on either side of them.

After a moment of silence, say the following:

- Pray in your heart for the person on your right. Ask God to bless and help him or her. Pray how the Holy Spirit leads you.

Allow a few moments of quiet.

- Now pray for the person on your left.

Leader: LORD of every moment, this is the day that you have made. We give you ourselves, and we ask you to use us and our gifts, that your people may draw closer to you. We make this prayer in the name of Jesus Christ our LORD. Amen.

Continuing to Gather Faithfully

Guiding Young People Beyond the Training

The Church Needs Young People

The purpose of *Gather Faithfully* is simple. It is to assist communities with training and integrating young people into the full life of the Eucharistic liturgy. They belong there because the Church needs young people. Consider the words of the late Pope John Paul II:

> We need the enthusiasm of the young. We need their joie de vivre. In it is reflected something of the original joy God had in creating man. The young experience this same joy within themselves. This joy is the same everywhere, but it is also ever new and original.
>
> (*Crossing the Threshold of Hope*, page 125)

Too often people say, "We need to make young people feel important." An examination of this statement reveals that it is flawed. Making young people "feel important" establishes far too low of a bar. It is patronizing and clashes with their dignity.

An honest examination of dispositions about young people may be in order. Regrettably, adults often make trite the contribution of young people, seeing their participation as, "neat," or (worse) "cute." Leaders of the Church, from the Holy Father, to local ordinaries, pastors, and campus ministers are recognizing that young people *are* important. As an advocate for young people, school campus ministers and parish youth leaders must make an opening for them in liturgical life, so that adults recognize that it is so much more than "neat" when young people take leadership roles within the Church but that their contribution is integral to a vibrant Catholic life.

Young People Need the Church

Jesus Christ is revealed in the Church. It is Jesus who washes us in the waters of Baptism. Jesus is heard in the proclamation. Jesus is seen in the community that gathers, and in the priest who offers the wine and the bread. Jesus forgives in the Sacrament of Reconciliation. He is received in the most Holy Eucharist. He blesses us with water. He calls us forth in prayer.

Young people crave truth and authenticity. They want to know that they matter, that their life matters. Their soul stirs at a deep place; the Church responds at a deep place. In the Eucharistic liturgy, young people find the depth, the truth, and the authenticity they crave.

For years, the question of youth ministry was, "What's the follow-up?" to whatever new program arose. The follow-up, of course is the Church herself. All programs, all ministry efforts must point to the Church herself, must leave young people "at the altar," so to speak, at the heartbeat of the Church. It is our Eucharistic and sacramental life that gives what it calls us toward, life on high with Christ Jesus.

"It is also necessary that the young know the Church, that they perceive Christ in the Church, Christ who walks through the centuries alongside each generation, alongside each person. He walks alongside each person as a friend" (Pope John Paul II, *Crossing the Threshold of Hope*, page 126). Often times that friendship is embodied by older members in the faith mentoring the younger members.

Though the *Gather Faithfully* sessions may be concluding, liturgical training never really does. As a mentor of young liturgical ministers, there are ongoing tasks:

1. The young people have been trained. Now they must be sent forth in the name of Jesus. Consult the *Book of Blessings* (Collegeville, MN: Liturgical Press, 1989):

- Chapter 61— Order for the Blessing of Readers
- Chapter 62—Order for the Blessing of Altar Servers, Sacristans, Musicians, and Ushers
- Chapter 63—Order for the Commissioning of Extraordinary Ministers of Holy Communion

This provides prayers and blessings for the blessing and commissioning of liturgical ministers. There are options included for within Mass or at a ceremony. Creating a meaningful celebration for your liturgical ministers will "place" them in the eyes of their community.

2. Continue the spiritual development of the liturgical ministers. Retreats, days of reflection, prayer helps, and resources are vital in helping liturgical ministers maintain a vibrant connection with Jesus in whose name they serve.

3. Continuing to build community among the liturgical ministers is also vital. It is easy for liturgical ministers to fall into thinking about "my" part of the liturgy, and lose sight of the mosaic that is the Catholic Eucharistic liturgy. When young people experience a personal connection with one another, it is easier for them to understand and value their connection in the liturgy as well.

4. Provide ongoing training and evaluation. Evaluation is most often interpreted as, "What do I need to tell them to fix?" Effective evaluation also

includes what is going well. The remarks about what is going well ought to be as specific as what needs to improve.

Closing

In Pope Benedict XVI's inaugural homily, he proclaimed: "Yes, the Church is alive . . . and the Church is young." By drawing young people into the very heart of the Eucharistic liturgy, they are being drawn into the person of Jesus Christ and his Body, the Church. The vitality of their worship will ensure that the Church will always be alive and will always be young!

Acknowledgments

The scriptural quotations contained herein are from the New Revised Standard Version of the Bible, Catholic Edition. Copyright © 1993 and 1989 by the Division of Christian Education of the National Council of the Churches of Christ in the United States of America. All rights reserved.

"The Grail Prayer" on page 44 is from *Walk in My Presence: A Book of Prayer Services and Themed Readings and Prayers,* by Nicholas Hutchinson (Chelmsford, England: Matthew James Publishing, 2000). Copyright © 2000 by Matthew James Publishing. Used with permission of the Grail (England) ©.

The quotation from the baptismal rite on page 51 is from *The Rites of the Catholic Church,* volume one, number 126 (Collegeville, MN: Liturgical Press, 1990), page 417. The English translation of *Rite of Baptism for Children,* copyright © 1969 (ICEL). Copyright © 1976, 1983, 1988, 1990 by Pueblo Publishing Company. Copyright © 1990 by the Order of Saint Benedict.

The prayer on page 62 is from *Manual of Prayers,* compiled by Reverend James D. Watkins (Chicago: Midwest Theological Forum, 1996), page 304. Copyright © 1996 by the American College of the Roman Catholic Church in the United States.

The excerpt on page 93 and the quotation on page 94 are from *Crossing the Threshold of Hope,* by John Paul II (New York: Alfred A. Knopf, 1994), pages 125 and 126. Copyright © 1994 by Arnoldo Mondadori Editore. Translation copyright © 1994 by Alfred A. Knopf.

The quotation by Pope Benedict XVI on page 95 is from *Homily of His Holiness Benedict XVI,* at *www.vatican.va/holy_father/benedict_xvi/ homilies/2005/documents/hf_ben-xvi_hom_20050424_inizio-pontificato _en.html,* accessed September 9, 2005.

To view copyright terms and conditions for Internet materials cited here, log on to the home pages for the referenced Web sites.

During this book's preparation, all citations, facts, figures, names, addresses, telephone numbers, Internet URLs, and other pieces of information cited within were verified for accuracy. The authors and Saint Mary's Press staff have made every attempt to reference current and valid sources, but we cannot guarantee the content of any source, and we are not responsible for any changes that may have occurred since our verification. If you find an error in, or have a question or concern about, any of the information or sources listed within, please contact Saint Mary's Press.